CHANCE

OR

CREATION?

CHANCE

— OR —

CREATION?

God's Design in the Universe

Attributed to
al-Jahiz
(AD 776–869)

Translated and introduced by
M. A. S. Abdel Haleem
School of Oriental and African Studies
University of London

Garnet
PUBLISHING

Chance or Creation?

Published by Garnet Publishing Limited
8 Southern Court
South Street
Reading
Berkshire, RG1 4QS, UK

Translation © M. A. S. Abdel Haleem 1995

First English edition

ISBN 1 85964 067 2

British Library Cataloguing-in-Publication Data.
A catalogue record for this book is available from
the British Library.

Jacket design by David Rose
Book design by David Rose
Illustrations by Nick Williams

Printed in the Lebanon

TABLE OF CONTENTS

✪ Contents ✪

Introduction

An old new question

Was it mere chance or the perfectly worked-out plan of God, the wise and powerful Creator, that brought about the universe? This question, which occupied the mind of the 9th-century author of this book, has been pondered on throughout history and is still being considered by philosophers, theologians and scientists today.

The notion of the world having come into existence by chance, therefore, is not a new one. The author targets those among the ancient Greeks who denied design in creation – but it is the Manichaeans who are of particular significance to him, these were followers of Mani, who was born about AD 215. Their refutations of Christian beliefs caused them to become the targets of Christian authors. However, the Manichaean philosophy spread and by the latter part of the 8th century they were also seen as a real threat to Islam and were in turn targeted by Muslim authors.

The author responds to the challenge from those who see only random chance in Creation, denying the presence of a divine power. He believes in a wise, powerful and benign Creator and sets out to present evidence for this belief. He does not, however, use the dry argument of the philosopher or the partisan dogma of a theologian. He does not dictate or preach, patronise or sermonise but continually

invites readers to 'Think of . . .', 'Reflect on . . .' and
'Look at . . .' matters for themselves and to re-examine
well-known facts. This gives the book a universal
appeal to sceptics and believers alike, in his age and
in our own time. Because his message was addressed
to non-believers as well as believers, he wisely bases
his arguments on evidence drawn from observing the
universe itself in the hope that 'it may serve as a cure
for the sceptics and rejectionists and that it would
strengthen the faith of believers'. Reflecting on such
matters as the rising and setting of the sun, the
provision in the natural world of medicinal herbs, the
design of the elephant's trunk and much more, the
author makes a comprehensive argument for design in
the universe.

His plan is clear and well-structured. He first looks
at the universe as a complete edifice, like a house,
then he goes on to deal with its different parts – the
sun and moon and other celestial bodies – before
looking at the creation of the Earth. He then deals
with plants, followed by animals before turning to
mankind. In the final part of the book, the author
tackles those philosophical arguments that deny
creation and design, such as why it should be that
God permits children to be born deformed and how
it can be that He allows disasters to affect anyone
regardless of whether they are good or bad. Such
arguments are still raised in our time and the

answers the author gives have an amazing
contemporary relevance over a thousand years after
they were first written.

Each section is discussed clearly and logically.
Dealing with the sun and moon, for example, he first
shows their effects on day and night, then on the
four seasons and then on the annual cycle. In
dealing with mankind he starts with the foetus, then
with the child and then goes on to the other stages of
development. Frequently he draws comparisons
between human beings, herbivores and carnivores to
illustrate his point, showing how the creation of each
suits their different functions or roles.

The author clearly delights in his observation of
natural phenomena, and in reflecting on their
implications. He frequently expresses wonder at the
abundance of creation and his exuberance is evident
throughout: 'Do you not see . . . ?' 'Why . . . ?' 'Why
not . . . ?' 'What if it were . . .' 'You may argue . . . ?'
'If you say so . . . we would answer . . .' 'Who made
this and that in this way?', as can be seen from this
example: 'Who made human beings male and female
other than He who created them to be reproductive?
Who made them reproductive other than He who
made them mortal? Who endowed them with tools of
work other than He who created them to work? Who
created them to work, other than He who made them

needy? Who inflicted need on them other than He who undertook to reform them? Who chose to endow only them with Reason other than He who ordained that they should be judged? Who gave them skills other than He who gave them possessions? Who provides them with all that their skills cannot achieve, other than He to whom sufficient gratitude cannot be shown? Glorious and Exalted is He; His bounties are numberless.'

The author considers the benefits of wind, water and plants and shows that everything, from the smallest moth or thorn to the widest expanse of desert and ocean space, has its place in the scheme of things.

He is honest and does not evade difficult questions. This is evident in the final part of the book where he counters the philosophical arguments against creation and design and leaves none unanswered. For instance, to those who state that death and extinction argue against the existence of a Creator, he says: 'But let us see the results which this proposition would lead to,' considering the implications for the planet if all human generations were to exist at the same time. He is confident of his arguments each of which ends with a firm conclusion. Even in those instances where the author accepts the arguments made by non-believers he does not accept the conclusions that they draw.

He argues for example, 'If half the things in the world made us uncertain as to its perfection, it would still be neither just nor proper behaviour to assume that the whole world was a matter of chance, because the appropriateness and perfection of the other half would prevent a hasty conclusion in this matter.' And to those who believe that science provides a better explanation, he points out the contradictions of their stance, 'It is amazing that some people who refuse to believe that a medication could be wrong, even though they see the doctors regularly making mistakes, believe that the world came into being by chance when they can see nothing accidental about it.'

The author sets out to show the evidence in the universe for a deliberate act of creation and design. He succeeds in putting a very powerful case and giving us, as he does so, a wonderful volume of inspirational writing.

The period of writing
The 9th century was a period of great intellectual activity in the Muslim world. Translation became increasingly important, particularly under the Abbasid Caliph Ma'moun (r. AD 813–33). The Syrian Christians were particularly active in translating material into Arabic, direct from Greek or through Syriac. Translations were also made from Persian

and Indian languages. Prompted by the Islamic teaching that 'knowledge is the lost property of the Muslim, and wherever he finds it he has most claim on it,' the Muslims readily accepted foreign knowledge, and the Greeks in particular were valued greatly.

This book, a product of that period, is widely attributed to the Muslim thinker, man of letters, theologian, and author of hundreds of books on all kinds of subjects, Abu Uthman Amr ibn Bahr al-Jahiz, who was born in Basra in AD 776 and died there in AD 868-9. Although al-Jahiz was born into a poor family he was interested in learning from his earliest days. His love for books was phenomenal – a voracious reader, he used to pay bookshop owners to allow him to be locked up in the shop to read at night. Al-Jahiz absorbed learning from all sources – Arabic, Greek, Persian, and Indian – and this is evident in his writing. He was a great humorist and polemicist, writing books in favour of and against the same subjects. He wrote, for instance, a book in praise of wine, another against wine; a book in praise of booksellers and one against booksellers. His encyclopaedic book on animals is a masterpiece on the subject in Arabic. So is his highly celebrated work *The Book of Misers*.

There is much in our text that points to it being the

work of al-Jahiz. It is known that he did write a book on the subject and certainly the subject-matter and sources were within the scope of his knowledge. There are also aspects of the language used which point to the text having been written by al-Jahiz. However, it does lack certain features commonly associated with al-Jahiz. There are also some who attribute the book to Jibril ibn Nuh, a Christian author, who is said to have written it during the time of the Abbasid Caliph al-Mutawakkil (r. AD 847–61). There is however internal evidence in the book in its present form which raises serious doubt about attributing it to Jibril ibn Nuh, although there is evidence that he had written a book on this theme. It was also said that other books on the same theme had been written in Greek by Christian Nestorians before Jibril, which were then translated into Syriac and Arabic, or were originally written in Syriac or Persian and then translated into Arabic. The author of our present text may well, therefore, have had examples before him, which he developed. The original idea and the inspiration for all these writings and the structural model, were clearly Greek.

The matter of the authorship will be discussed more fully in the Arabic edition of the text, and should not detain us here. Our intention in this edition is to give the reader a chance to read this text in English, as an example of how enriching the contacts

between cultures were and are. Here we have a text,
the original inspiration for which comes from
classical Greek, which was developed in turn by
Christians, and Muslims, and is now translated into
a modern European language.

In a time where we speak of a 'Global Village', this
book addresses concerns shared by people of
different cultures and ages, using reasoned
arguments and evidence, accessible to everyone.
It is a classic work of liberal thinking, exemplifying
the qualities of honesty and interest in different
points of view.

At a time when there is growing holistic concern for
the environment, this book illustrates how
everything in the universe is interconnected with a
role or function within a finely balanced system and
how disturbance to one part of this system will upset
the whole. In our age of growing inter-faith
discussion, it is hoped that this book will show how
many beliefs, values and approaches are shared by
us all.

ONE

The Universe and the Organisation of its Parts

In the name of God, the Beneficent, the Merciful. May He bless Prophet Muhammad and his family and all other prophets.

Some people, unaware of the cause and meaning of created things, and failing to reflect on the perfection and wisdom evident in Creation, have fallen into denial and rejection, to the extent that they have denied that things were created, and have claimed that they came about at random, without craftsmanship or due calculation. Such people are like blind men who enter a perfectly built house, provided with the best furniture and all manner of food and drink and whatever is to be desired, with everything correctly arranged according to a perfect plan. They walk through the house unable to see its shape or furnishings. Should one of them stumble against something put in its place for a specific purpose of which he was unaware, he might well grumble resentfully and criticise both the house and the one who built it.

Such is the situation of the kind of people who deny Creation. As their minds are closed to the knowledge of the reasons and purpose of things, they wander in this world like men perplexed and cannot see the perfection in Creation, and the appropriate forms it takes. Should one of them stumble on something, being ignorant of its reason and purpose, he will hasten to condemn it and find faults and inconsistencies in it, as did the Manichaeans and other people in error and disbelief.

Thus anyone whom God has blessed with knowing the Creator – anyone who has been enabled to reflect on Creation and realise its subtle design and perfect proportion, from the evidence that exists in the Creation – has a duty to reveal unstintingly what has come to his knowledge through such reflection. Indeed he must work strenuously to publicise such knowledge and broadcast it to the hearing and minds of others, so that their causes for belief may be strengthened and the intrigues of the Devil to mislead their fancies may be foiled. In doing this a person should count on reward from God and be sure of His aid and support in his task.

We have therefore collected together all the signs and evidence that the world was created with composition, harmony and perfect planning which we have been guided to comprehend. We have explained in this book, as far as our knowledge goes, the reasons for all this and what it means, aiming to make it so plain and brief that it may be easy to understand and close to our readers' way of thinking, in the hope that it may serve as a cure for sceptics and rejectionists, and that it will strengthen the faith of those who are rightly guided. May God guide us in our task.

The first lesson is in the particular form of this universe and how its components are put together and organised. If you reflect on the universe you will find it like a house that has been built and equipped with all that is necessary. The sky is raised high like a ceiling, the earth is spread out like a carpet and the stars arranged like lamps or jewels stored in their settings like treasures. Everything has its place and purpose. Man is like the owner of the house who has authority over its contents. All manner of plants are provided for his needs and various animals are set to work for his benefit. In all this there is clear evidence that the universe was created according to a plan, with purpose and order, and that its Creator is the One who combined the different parts and arranged them. Scholars of the past have talked sufficiently about this but we will look at another aspect of the subtlety of Creation to explain its rightness, wisdom, order and suitability. This will serve to discredit those who believe that it is left to chance and those who believe in two opposite origins. Chance could not produce correctness and opposing forces could not produce order.

The colour of the sky

Reflect on the colour of the sky and its appropriateness. This particular colour is not only the one most suitable for the sight but also gives it strength. For those with impaired vision physicians prescribe frequent scanning of darkening shades of green. For those with fatigued vision, skilful physicians prescribe staring at a green basin full of water. Consider how the surface of the sky has these darkening shades of green, to attract eyes that look at it without harming them by looking too long. What people have learned through reflection and experience can be found already supplied in the Creation.

The rising and setting of the sun

Consider how the rising and setting of the sun maintains the domains of night and day. If it did not rise, the world would become unworkable. If the world was engulfed in darkness, how would people go about for their business, earn their living and move about as they desire? How could they enjoy living without having the joy and comfort of light? The benefits of the rising of the sun are quite obvious and need no elaboration. But reflect on the benefits in the setting of the sun. Without its setting, people would not obtain the rest and calm they badly need to relax their bodies and reinvigorate their senses, or that power which digests food and sends it to the different limbs of the body in the way

described in medical texts. Moreover, lust for money
would lead people to continue working in a way that
would harm their bodies. Many people in their
eagerness to gather wealth, would not stop were it
not for the coming of darkness at nightfall. Besides,
the earth would become too hot under the
continuous shining of the sun, and this would burn
every animal and plant on its surface. By Divine
arrangement, the sun shines for some of the time
and sets at other times, like a lamp which is put up
in a house for a while so that people may do what is
necessary, then is taken away so that they will have
rest and calm. Thus darkness and light, opposite as
they are, cooperate in a way that is useful for the
world and sustains it.

The movement of the sun: the four seasons and the yearly cycle

Then consider the ascent and decline of the sun
regulating the four seasons of the year and the
benefits in these. In winter the heat in trees and
plants decreases, and the fruit germs are generated;
the air becomes dense causing clouds and rain. The
bodies of animals become strong and so does natural
activity. In the spring nature is set in motion and the
elements which germinated in the winter appear,
producing plants, and blossoms in the trees.
Animals are moved to copulate. In the summer the
air becomes hot; heat ripens the fruit, melts away

the excesses in the body, and dries the surface of the earth ready for building and other activities. In the autumn the air becomes purer so that diseases are relieved, the body becomes healthier and night-time becomes longer, making it possible for prolonged activity to take place at night. There are many other benefits in addition to these which it would take too long to count.

Reflect on the movement of the sun through the signs of the Zodiac, how it sets up the annual cycle, and the benefits in such Divine arrangements. It is this cycle that includes the four seasons, winter, spring, summer and autumn, bringing them all to completion; and within this measure of the solar cycle, produce and fruit come to full ripeness and goodness, after which the whole cycle of beginning and growth will be resumed. The Ancients were right to say that time is a measurement of motion. We see that the year measures the motion of the sun from Aries to Aries. By the year and its parts we can measure time and periods, from the time God created the world to every succeeding time and age and by it people also measure their ages and times appointed for debts, hiring and other dealings. By the motion of the sun the year is completed and the calculation of time is given exact measurement.

The motion of the moon and determination of months

In this there is a clear, sublime indication of divine planning. Common people use it to determine the month. The calculation of the year cannot be done according to the moon because its cycle does not fall equally within the four seasons, or the germination and development of fruits. For that reason the lunar month and year lag behind the solar month and year, and the lunar month moves gradually: sometimes it is in winter and sometimes in summer.

The distribution of sunlight

Reflect on the rising of the sun over the world, and how it is planned. If it were made to rise in one spot in the sky and stand there, not going beyond it, its rays would not reach many mountains because they would have been blocked by other mountains and obstructions. By the ordinance of God it rises in the East at the beginning of the day and shines on things facing it in the West, then it moves, covering one area after another until it reaches the West, and shines on what was hidden from it at the beginning of the day. Thus there is no place left which does not receive its share of the sun.

The length of day and night and their effects

Reflect on the length of night and day and how they were established in a way beneficial to Creation.

The maximum length of each of them is fifteen hours, and no more. Just think: if the length of the day were one or two hundred hours, would that not result in the perishing of animals and plants on the surface of the earth? Animals would not calm down and stop working throughout that time, nor would cattle stop feeding as long as they could see the light of the day, nor would man stop working and moving about. They would all become exhausted and come to destruction. As for plants, they would burn and wither under the heat and glare of the sun. Similarly, if the night-time were to extend equally long, it would stop various animals from moving about and going out to feed until they perished with hunger, and the natural heat would be reduced in plants so that they would rot and perish. We see the same with plants which are shaded from the sun.

The light from the moon and stars

Consider the light of the moon and stars and their value in the darkness of the night. Although there is a need for darkness, so that animals may settle down and the air over plants become cool, it would not be good to have utterly dense darkness at night, without light so that it would not be possible to work; since people may need to work at night, either because they do not have sufficient time for some tasks during the day, or because intense heat makes it necessary to carry out work by moonlight, such as ploughing the field or making bricks or cutting wood. Moonlight at night enables people to do such work when necessary. The rising of the moon in only a part of the night, and the fact that its light is less than that of the sun, were so ordained that men do not persist in working as they do during the day and refrain from repose and rest so that they become exhausted. Some lights were made in the form of the stars to substitute for that of the moon when it is absent, and to enable some necessary movement. In emergencies which require escaping from danger or moving in the darkness of the night, if there were no light at all people would not be able to move from one place to another. Reflect on the subtle wisdom of this arrangement, where darkness has its proper domain and duration as needed, and yet within that time there is still some light for the needs we have described.

The stars and their varying movements

There are other benefits in the stars. They are signs and guides to the timing of many activities such as agriculture and planting, journeying on land and on sea, and also natural occurrences such as wind, heat and cold. Thus, those journeying at night can be guided through the desolate desert and tumultuous seas. In addition, they are signs of the power of the Creator who ordained their movements, their rising and setting. The movement of the moon in

particular, especially its appearance as a crescent at
the beginning of the month, its last phases, its
waxing, waning and eclipse, are all established for
the proper regulation of the world.

Deduction shows us that these luminous objects
move at great speed since they circle, in a day and a
night, one full circle and return to their starting
place to rise. Were it not for that great speed they
could not have covered this vast distance in twenty-
four hours. Think: if the sun and stars were so near
to us that we were able to apprehend their speed as
it is, would they not dazzle the sight with their rays
and glare, just as we sometimes experience when
lightning recurs frequently, quivering in the sky?
Similarly, if we imagined people in a dome studded
with lamps which revolved round them at speed,
would this not dazzle their sight and make them look
away? Reflect, then, how it was ordained that these
objects should move at that vast distance away from
us so that they may not harm our sight, and at a
great speed so that they may not lag behind the time
set for them.

Reflect on those stars that can be seen during one
part of the year and are hidden during others, such
as the Pleiades, Gemini and Sirius. If they were
made to appear and disappear all together at one
and the same time, none of them would individually

possess the indications known to people now, which guide them in some of their affairs, such as they find in the rising and setting of the Pleiades and Gemini. The rising and setting of each of them at its own proper time is made to guide people in specific matters. Just as the Pleiades, for some good end, were made to appear at one time and disappear at others, Ursa Major and Minor were made not to disappear for a different one. They are like landmarks which show people unknown routes on land and sea, since they never set or disappear and people look at them when they wish, and are guided by them to their destinations. The two types, variant as they are, both bring benefits and satisfy different needs.

The orbits of the celestial bodies

Reflect on the stars and the various ways in which they move. One group maintains its place in orbit, moving only slightly and all together; another group moves through the signs of the Zodiac and its members disperse on their ways, each one of them moving along two different paths, the first, together with the general orbit, towards the West, and another particular to itself, towards the East. People in the past compared this free type of star to an ant moving on a millstone, with the millstone rotating towards the right while the ant rotates towards the left. Hence the ant moves in two different directions: its own forward motion and, compelled by the stone,

pulled backwards. We should ask those who claim
that stars developed their characteristics by chance,
without deliberation on the part of a Creator, 'What
prevented them from being all stationary or all
moving? Since chance postulates only one single
possibility. How did it produce two different motions
to a specific measure and order? Surely these two
types of movement indicate deliberation and order,
not chance as claimed by those who deny the power
and ordination of God?'

If you ask why some stars were established as
stationary and others as moving, we answer: if they
were all stationary, we would not have the
indications derived from the movement of those that
move, and from the fact that they fall into one sign of
the Zodiac for a limited time, just as we derive
indications for things happening in the world from
the movement of the sun, the moon and stars
through their stations. If, on the other hand, they
were all moving, their movement would have had no
recognisable stations, nor would there be any
standard by which to measure it, since we measure
the motion of those that move by their passage into
the stationary signs, just as we measure the motion
of a person on earth by the houses he passes by. In
short, if they were all in the same orbit, their
arrangement would be disrupted and the advantages
would not be obtained. A person could then say that

13

their uniform state would mean that they had been
produced by chance as we have explained. The
differentiation of their movements with its practical
advantages is the clearest evidence of deliberation
and organisation.

Reflect: why should this sphere, with its sun, moon,
stars and signs revolve round the world in this
continuous manner, with this precision and
proportion, were it not for the fact that – in the
alternation of night and day, and the four seasons of
the year, over the earth and the animals and plants
that live on it – there are all those advantages which
we have listed and clarified above? Could any
reasoning person fail to see that this is an
arrangement of wise and just proportion, ordained
by a Wise Designer?

If you say that this arrangement is something that
just happened, what would prevent you from saying
the same about a water-wheel which you observe
turning to irrigate a garden with its plants and trees?
You see that everything in the machine is designed
to fit together in a way that benefits the garden and
its contents. How could you prove your view if you
declared it? What would people say to you when
they heard it, other than to dismiss your opinion as
stupid and your mind as deranged? Would you then
deny saying that a humble water-wheel, constructed

with ingenuity for the benefit of a small piece of
land, was made without a maker who designed it,
and yet dare to say the same thing about the greatest
wheel, created with wisdom that exceeds that of the
human mind, for the benefit of all the earth and
what it contains: that it chanced to happen without
making and design? If that sphere fell into disrepair,
as water-wheels do, men would have no means of
repairing it; and if it was out of order for a year or
part of a year, what state would they be in, and how
would they continue to live? Do you not see how
people have been spared such a terrible situation
which they would have no means of correcting? And
the sphere turns on its way without any disrepair, its
benefits and uses never failing, without any
irregularity in its time cycle – all for the sake of the
efficiency of the universe and everything it contains.

Heat and cold and their measured alternation in the world

Consider heat and cold and their characteristic
alternation in the world, increasing and decreasing
and arriving at a moderate temperature in order to
maintain the four seasons of the year and the
benefits inherent in them. Moreover, they tan the
body to keep it in good condition. Were it not for the
alternate action of heat and cold on the body, it
would deteriorate, its strength would diminish and it
would decay very quickly. Then think how heat and

15

cold displace each other, at a gradual, leisurely pace. You must notice how one decreases gradually while the other increases, until each of them reaches its maximum limits of gain and loss. If either one, heat or cold, were to come suddenly after the other, that would harm the body and weaken it, just as leaving a hot bath for an excessively cold atmosphere would do. Such a gentle rate of climatic change was created only to keep us safe from the harm of sudden change. Why should this be so, if it were not by the arrangement of a Designer?

If you claim that this gentle interchange of heat and cold is so because of the slow movement of the sun in its rising and setting, I shall ask you the reason for the slow movement of the sun. If you explain that slow movement by the vast distance between East and West, you will be asked about the cause for that phenomenon, and questions will continue to be posed however far you pursue the argument, until you finally concede that there is deliberation and design. Were it not for the heat, hard, bitter fruits would not ripen and become soft and sweet so that we enjoy eating them, fresh or dried. Were it not for the cold, plants would not sprout and reproduce, or produce abundant enough crops, some for people to eat and some to return to the ground. Do you not appreciate the great advantages of having heat and cold – how indispensable they are? Both of them, even with all these advantages, and even though they are indispensable, can cause pain and weakness in the body. This is the way in which you should look at many things which cause discomfort, and which do not seem to suit people's desires, although they are wisely designed for their benefit.

The wisdom of creating fire

Just reflect on the wisdom of the Creator and His design in the creation of fire, and how it behaves. It would not have been appropriate for fire to be spread around like air and water, as it would burn the world and all that is in it; however, it was necessary for it to appear sometimes because of its many advantages. It was therefore made as if 'stored in' the substances that contain it. It can be kindled at need to ignite the fuel for as long as we need it, after which it will subside. It does not burn in the substance and the fuel all the time, so as to cause harm, nor is it spread about in the world to burn everything in its path. Thus it was made in such a form and measure as to give us the benefits while sparing us the harm.

There is a further feature of fire: it is restricted to man out of all the animals, for good reasons. If man were deprived of fire the damage and discomfort in his life would be great, but animals neither use fire

17

nor enjoy it. Because all this was intended to be so, man was given a palm and fingers suitable for striking sparks and using fire. Animals were not given these features but were equipped with endurance in discomfort, hardship and deprivation, so that they might not suffer as man would from lack of fire.

I must further draw your attention to one small benefit of fire which is yet very significant: the lamp, which people use to enable them to continue at night to fulfil their needs as they wish. Without lamps, people would have spent half their lives as though in the grave. Who could write, or learn, or copy in the darkness of the night? What would be the state of someone who had an attack of pain at night, and needed to tie a bandage, or take some medicine? As for the blessing of fire in cooking food, warming the body, drying certain things, melting others, and such other benefits, they are too many to count, and too obvious not to be noticed.

The wind

Consider the breeze which we call wind, and the great lessons and benefits in it. It maintains bodies: we breathe it to stay alive, and it refreshes us outwardly. It carries sound to great distances, and it carries fragrance from one place to another. Consider how a smell arrives from the direction of

the wind, and likewise a sound. Wind carries the
alternation of heat and cold to the benefit of the
whole world. Wind refreshes bodies, carries clouds
from place to place to spread their good effects,
gathers them together so that they become dense,
causing rain, then disperses them, causing dry
weather in which trees grow and pollinate. Ships are
propelled by it. It is used to winnow, to cool water, to
intensify fire and to dry wet things. In short, it gives
life to everything on earth. But for the wind, plants
would wither, animals would die, objects would
become mouldy and rot. Do you not see how, when
there is a dead calm, it causes stuffiness and
distress to people and animals? It makes the healthy
sick, and the sick moribund. It spoils fruits, it rots
pulses, and leads to plagues in bodies and pests in
crops. All this demonstrates that the blowing of the
wind on most days is by wise design and planning
for the benefit of all creatures.

Let me point out a further quality of air. Sound, as
scholars teach, is the effect of striking objects in the
air, which the air then carries to people's ears.
People talk about their needs and dealings all day
long and part of the night. If the effect of all this talk
were to remain in the air, as writing remains on
paper, the world would have been saturated with it
to our distress and great harm; to change and
replace all this would take much more than to

replace writing on paper, because the amount of speech that remains unwritten is many times that which is written. But the All-Knowing Creator has made this air a hidden sheet of paper. It carries our words for as long as necessary; then they are erased and the sheet becomes blank again: without any effort or resolve on our part it nevertheless ceaselessly carries whatever we load it with.

TWO

The Creation
of the Earth

Think of the creation of this earth, and how it was made steady and stable, so that it is possible to walk and settle on it. People and cattle can walk around on it as necessary, sit down to rest and lie down to sleep, and they can also complete their work. If the earth were made shaky or unstable, people would not be able to complete their building, carpentry, metalwork, or sewing: in fact they would have no comfort in a life where the earth was shaking beneath them. Compare this with what happens to people during even very short-lived earthquakes: they flee out of their houses. If you ask, 'Why should the earth quake?' we will say that earthquakes and other such things exist in order to strike fear into people, so that they turn to God and desist from sins. Likewise other afflictions that happen to their bodies or their fortunes – calamities and famines – are ordained to lead to their correction. If they reform, rewards and compensation far superior to anything in this world are stored up for them in the Hereafter. Sometimes these are given to them in this world if it is deemed to be for their good and benefit.

If the earth is cool and solid by nature, so are stones. The difference is in the greater solidity of stones. Think: if the solidity of the earth were to be increased until it became like rock, could it produce those plants which give life to all animals? How would it be possible to plough it or seed it, or erect buildings? Do you not see that it was made less firm than stones and soft enough to be suitable for various activities? Another example of wise design in the creation of earth is that the wind blows from the north, and the north is higher than the south. This phenomenon enables water to flow down the surface of the earth to irrigate and water it, ending in the sea, just as one raises one edge of a surface, and lowers the other so that the water will flow down it and not stand and spoil it. The same is true of the upland north and lowland south: otherwise the water would remain standing on the surface of the earth and thus stop people from their work and cut off their routes and roads.

The mountains

Look at the mountains, made of heaped up mud and stone. The thoughtless might think they are redundant, without use, while in fact they have many beneficial properties. Snow falls on them and remains on their peaks for those who need it in the summer. Some melts, giving rise to a profusion of springs that gather to make great rivers which in turn nurture all kinds of plants and herbs that do not grow on the plains. In the mountains there are also caves and lairs for hunting animals and other wild creatures. Fortresses and impregnable castles are built on them to foil the enemy. Stones are hewn from them for building and grinding. There are also mines in them for all sorts of valuable minerals. There may well be other qualities known only to Him who planned them in His foreknowledge.

Mines and quarries

Reflect on mines and quarries and the valuable minerals that come out of them, such as gypsum and lime, arsenic and vitriol, cement, zinc, silver and gold, chrysolite, ruby, mercury, copper, lead, silicates, tar, pitch, sulphur, oil and other substances people use in their necessities and luxuries, and how different they are in their natures, colours, conditions. Some are deadly poisons, some antidotes, some increase or remove the effects of others. Can any rational person be blind to the fact that these are all treasures stored in the earth for man to extract and use for his needs?

In addition, reflect on the rarity of gold and silver and the incapacity of all man-made methods to manufacture them, no matter how zealous and industrious people may be. Were anyone to discover a way of making precious metals, it would become known to everybody. Then gold and silver would become abundant and lose their value, so that they would be useless for buying and selling, dealing, paying taxes to rulers, or storing as assets. Yet people were given the skill to make alum from

copper, glass from sand, and other harmless things.
Think how they were granted what they wanted in
matters that incur no harm, and were denied in
matters that would harm them. We have been told by
some who work in mines that they have dug deep
until they reached a spot where they could
apparently see mountains of silver, but before them
there was a great gulf, filled with flowing, bottomless
water with no way across. They returned to find it
but could not, and departed in sorrow. Reflect on
this design of the Creator. He wished to show these
miners His power and His great treasures so that
they would know that if He wanted to grant them
mountains of silver, He could have done so, but it
would be of no benefit to them, since such quantities
would decrease the value of this metal. Compare the
way in which unusual products – pots or other such
articles of furniture – have great value when rare,
but lose worth and value when plentiful. There is
truth in the saying that the value of things lies in
their rarity.

Abundance of the four elements
Think of the abundance God has created in the four
elements to satisfy all the demands people make on
them. First if the expanse and extent of the earth
were not so great, how could it be wide enough to
accommodate all the dwellings of men, their
plantations, pastures, crops, fuel-woods, efficacious

medicinal herbs and useful minerals? You may object to vast empty places and desolate deserts and say, 'What use are they?' but have you forgotten that they are dwelling-places and pastures for wild animals, besides enabling humans to leave their homes when they need a change. Many an empty desert has developed palaces and gardens through men moving into it. Without the widespread expanse of land, men would be as if besieged in an enclosed place, unable to leave even when under compulsion.

Likewise if water did not run in springs and streams and flow in rivers, there would not be enough of it for men to drink, water their cattle, animals, plants, trees, and all kinds of crops, as well as for the wild beasts and birds and game to drink, and for all the fish and marine creatures. The same with the air: were it not for its abundance, creatures would suffocate in smoke and steam, which would not gradually turn into mists and clouds. The same with fire: although it is not found everywhere, it is there within certain substances, stored up against various needs for the reasons we have explained earlier.

Let me remind you of the benefits of water of which you are aware, though heedless of their significance. In addition to the great purpose of keeping every animal and plant on earth alive, it mixes with juices to dilute them to a suitable taste; it cleans the body and other things when they get dirty; it moistens the soil and makes it suitable for use; it quenches fire, when it might cause great harm; it saves a choking person from death; a tired person bathes in water to find comfort for the limbs, and there are many other benefits, the importance of which we realise when they are needed. If you doubt the usefulness of that great volume of water accumulated in the seas, and say 'What is the benefit of that?' I would remind you that it is the habitat and area of activity for countless types of fish and marine animals; it is the source of pearls, coral, ruby, ambergris and other marine produce. On its shores grow varieties of aloes, wood and fragrant and medicinal herbs. Moreover it is used to transport people and all kinds of trade from faraway places, for instance from China to Iraq, and from Iraq to China. If such wares were carried only on the backs of people and animals, they would become unsaleable, and would remain in their places of origin in the possession of their first owners, because the costs of carrying them would be far greater than their value. Nobody would then bother to carry them, with two results: the loss to many places of many things that people need, and loss of livelihood to those who transport and trade in them.

The falling of the rain; its alternation with fair weather
Reflect on the falling of the rain and the design in it.

27

It is so made as to fall on the ground to cover rough, high land and irrigate it. If it were made to come from one side only, it would not reach the higher places and cultivated land would be reduced, for we can see that irrigated land is less than the total of that which is cultivated. Rain falls down on the ground and waters the open spaces, mountain slopes and heights, which produce plentiful crops. It saves people in many parts of the world the trouble of moving water from one place to another, and prevents the resultant miserliness and quarrels which make the mighty and powerful monopolise the water and deprive the weak. When it was designed to fall down on the ground, it was made in drops like spray so that it would sink into the earth and irrigate it. If it had been poured on the surface it would fail to sink, thus damaging the standing plants. It was made, therefore, to fall gently and enable the seeds to grow and the standing plants to thrive. In the falling of rain there are also other benefits, for it moistens the body and clears the dust from the air, preventing diseases that could arise from dust. It washes the trees and plants clean from diseases, and there are many other such benefits. If you say, 'Is it not true that in some years it can cause great harm by pouring in torrents or hailstones that smash the crops, or make the air thick and cause many diseases in the body and pests in crops?' we answer, 'Yes, this could happen, but there is some advantage for people in that it prevents them from sinning, and from persisting in sin. The benefit which they receive in correcting their religious life is higher than the harm that befalls their wealth.'

Reflect on how the rain and sunshine alternate in the world in a beneficial way. If either was constant, that would harm the world. Do you not appreciate that continuous rain rots vegetables and pulses, saps the strength of animals' bodies, thickens the air, causing various diseases and ruins roads and pathways? On the other hand, when fair weather persists, bodies and plants dry up, fruits take longer to ripen, water subsides in springs and valleys, a phenomenon that brings harm to people by drying the air and causing various diseases. However, if they alternate the air becomes cleansed and each averts the harm of the other so that everything is kept in a healthy state.

If you say, 'Why should there be any harm at all in either of them?' we would answer: 'This would disturb and cause people some discomfort and pain so that they become mindful of, and desist from, sins.' When a person's body becomes sick, it needs bitter medicine to cure and restore it. Likewise, if a man becomes tyrannical and insolent he needs something to disturb and cause him pain, to bring him to his senses and make him desist from his bad ways and do right. If a king were to divide tons of gold and silver amongst the people of his kingdom, would they not consider this great generosity, and would not his fame reach far and wide? How little is such bounty compared to one spell of rain which covers the whole land and increases the value of crops by tons of gold and silver in all regions of the earth. Do you not see that although one spell of rain is so great a good, and the blessing of God so all-encompassing towards them, human beings take no notice? It may, of course, prevent someone from going out for some business. If he resents this, he prefers something small to something much greater.

THREE

Plants

Reflect on the plants and the benefits we have from them: crops for food, straw for fodder, stems for fuel, and wood for all kinds of carpentry; bark and leaves; flowers and stems; branches and resins for all kinds of benefits. Think how much trouble it would cause us if all the crops on which we feed were to be found heaped on the ground, instead of carried on the stems and branches of plants. Would they be in good condition if they were heaped on the ground? There is great benefit and wisdom in their being designed as they are: the great benefit of fuel, of foliage and straw would be lost if food were to be found on the ground. There is also joy in observing the plants and their freshness unequalled by any other spectacle or entertainment in the world. Glory be to Him Who created everything in the best possible way!

Abundance in production

Reflect further on the yield produced by the earth, where one grain may produce a hundred grains more or less, when it would have been possible for each grain to produce just one. Why were they made so abundant, if not to be enough for some to fall back into the ground, and others to feed the farmer and other people? Do you not recognise that when a king wishes to populate a land, his method is to give people seeds to sow and to feed them until they harvest? Reflect how we find this in the design of the Wise Creator, who made plants produce such abundant crops for food and cultivation. The same with trees and palm trees. You find that each root has around it many saplings. Why was it so made, if not to provide enough for people to cut some down and use them for whatever they need, and leave others to keep the plantation going? If each root were to remain single without producing saplings or crops, it would not be possible to cut anything for any use at all, or to replant. If a pest were to attack it, that would be the end of its existence.

The protection of seeds

Think of the plants, of the seeds of lentils, beans, and watercress, and similar plants. They grow in pods or containers like pockets, to protect and shield them from pests until they become strong, just like the uterine sac around the foetus, which was made for the same purpose. As for wheat and similar grains they grow in rows, in hard husks with spikes on top, similar to spearheads, to protect them from the birds. If you say, 'But birds can still get at some of these grains,' I would say, 'Yes, indeed they can. Birds were also created by God, and He has given them a share in what the earth produces; but grains are fortified in this way so that the birds do not utterly demolish them, and destroy the crops.' If grains were exposed and uncovered, birds would decimate them, with the result that they would

overfeed and might die, and the farmer would gain
nothing from his plantation. Those husks were made
so that the birds would take a little for feed, but
most of it would remain for man: he is more worthy
of it, since it was he who sowed and watered it, and
he needs more than the birds.

Trees

Consider the wisdom in the creation of trees and
various plants. Since, like animals, they need
continuous nourishment, but are without mouths
like animals or the ability to move, their roots are
fixed in the soil so that they can draw nourishment
from it, to send it to the branches, leaves and fruits
they bear. Thus the earth is like a nursing mother to
them and their roots are like mouths which fasten on
to the earth to draw nourishment as young animals
suckle from their mothers.

Consider how the posts that support large and small
tents are supported by ropes on all sides so that they
remain vertical, without falling or tilting over.
Likewise you find that all plants have roots spread
in the earth, extending in all directions to fix them
and keep them upright. If it were not so, how could
lofty palms and mighty trees remain standing in the
face of storms?

Consider how the craft in Creation preceded that

used in manufacture. The craft used in manufacture
to support tents came later, for trees were created
much earlier and the poles and supports of tents all
come from trees. The Ancients spoke truly when
they said that craft imitates nature.

Leaves, kernels and stones

Consider the creation of leaves. You will find that all
of them have something like veins spread
throughout the leaf, some of them thick, going along
the leaf and across it, while others are fine,
intersecting these thick ones and interwoven in a
remarkable pattern. If they were hand-made like
human crafts one leaf of one tree could not be
completed within a whole year! Nor need anyone stir
abroad, use tools, craft or energy, yet within a few
days of Spring you find leaves appearing in such
vast numbers that they cover the mountains, valleys
and all the earth without anyone moving or speaking
except, that is, for the Divine Will which operates
in everything!

Consider the reason for these veins. They are made
to spread throughout the leaf to provide water and to
transport nutrients, just as human veins spread
throughout the body to transport nourishment to
every part of it. Another point about the large veins
– the thick ones – their solidity supports the leaf so
that it may not be pierced or torn. A leaf is clearly

similar to a kite made by craftsmen from pieces of fabric, with sticks fixed lengthwise and widthwise to keep it stiff. Although we have used an example from craft to explain nature, nature actually came first.

Consider kernels and stones and the wisdom in them. They are distributed inside the fruits to perform the function of planting, in case no actual planting should take place. In the same way we store precious objects which we badly need in many places so that, if something happens to some of them in one place, we can still find others elsewhere. Moreover, with their hardness, kernels support the softness and delicateness of the fruit so that it does not break, or fall apart, or decay. Some stones are nuts that can be eaten or from which useful oil can be extracted.

Now that you have seen the wisdom in kernels and stones, consider the food that covers them, such as the dates on their stones and the flesh of the grapes covering the pips. Why do they come in this form when it is possible instead to have something inedible as we see in cypress, plane and tamarisk, and other trees? Why are they covered with such delicious nourishment if not for the enjoyment of human beings, animals and pests?

Perennial cycle of death and revival in trees
Consider another aspect of design in trees. You find
them dying once a year but natural warmth is
retained inside and the raw material of fruits
gestates. The trees then revive and spread and
produce one type of fruit after another, just as
varieties of hand-made sweets are presented to you
one after the other. You will notice that the branches
present you with fruits as if they were handing them
over and the flowers on their branches exhibit
themselves to you as if in greeting. Who would have
arranged all this but a Wise Creator who determines
all? What other possible reason could there be for
such diversity, other than for the delight of humans?
Are you not astonished that people meet the Creator
with ingratitude rather than thankfulness for His
blessings?

The pomegranate
Consider the shape of the pomegranate, and the
indications of design and purposefulness therein.
You will find inside mounds of a white, fat-like
substance studded with pips as if they had been
arranged by hand. These pips are divided into
clusters, each of them enclosed in a tissue woven in
the most marvellous and delicate fashion. The skin
of the pomegranate covers it all. The marvellous
design of this shape demands that the skin is not
filled just with pips, since the pips would not feed

each other. The fat-like substance is fashioned to surround the pips to provide them with nourishment, for we see the root of each pip is fixed in it. The pips are wrapped in the tissue which contains and supports them so that they do not shake. Over all this comes the hard skin to preserve the fruit and protect it from pests. These are just a few examples out of many in the description of a pomegranate. Much more could be observed by those who want to go on longer, but what we have said contains teaching enough.

Gourds
Consider how the weak gourd vine can carry such heavy fruits as calabash, cucumber, melon, and the wisdom in this. Since it was designed to carry such fruits, the plant was made to lie flat on the ground. Had it been made to stand vertically like many plants and trees, it would not be able to bear such fruits, and it would break down before they reached maturity. Consider how it was made to spread across the surface of the ground so that it can rest its burden there: you see the plant of marrow or water melon spread across the ground with its fruits spread around it, as if it were a female cat stretched out with its kittens round it, suckling. And consider how these varieties of fruit come at the most suitable time of high summer and intense heat, so that our nature greets them with joy and longs for them. Were

they to arrive in winter they would have been met
with shudders of distaste. They would also have
been harmful to the body. Remember that sometimes
cucumbers arrive in winter and people refrain from
eating them, unless they are so greedy that they do
not refrain from eating what harms them.

Palm trees

Consider a special feature of palm trees. Since there
are females that need fertilisation there are also
created males to fertilise them. A male tree is like a
male animal which fertilises females that carry
offspring while he does not. Consider also the
creation of the palm-trunk. It is woven of criss-
crossed fibres like the warp and weft we make by
hand, so that the trunk becomes sturdy and does not
break under the weight of the heavy crown or the
blowing of stormy winds, and is ready to be used as
timber for ceilings, bridges and other such uses. The
same with wood, which is woven vertically and
horizontally like the muscle-fibre of meat. What is
more, it is so sturdy as to be suitable for use in
making tools. Had it been as hard as stone it would
not be possible to use it for ceilings and other uses
such as doors, beds, boxes and so on.

One of the great benefits of wood, well known to
everybody, is that it floats on water, although not
everybody knows all the varieties of benefits derived

from this characteristic. Were it not able to float how could ships and rafts carry mountains of cargo? How could people replace its function of making it easy to carry on trade from one land to another? It would have been so difficult for them to transport things, that the abundance of one land would be totally lacking, or rarely found, in another.

Medicinal herbs

Consider medicines and how each of them is designed to cure a specific ailment. One, like *lapidion* (pepperwort), sinks into the joints to extract from them the thick residue; another, like *apithimon* (wild thyme) extracts the black bile; another, like *sagapinon* (root of *ferula persica*) sweetens the breath; yet another, like *ippomarathon* (horse fennel), dissolves swellings, and there are many besides. Who put these properties in them, if not the One who created them for their uses; and who made human beings discover their properties if not the One who endowed them with such? How long would it have taken to stumble upon this by accident, as some have argued. Human beings were given the understanding to grasp through their minds and penetrating thought. Who made animals understand the effects of such medicines, so that some seek treatment from certain medicines for wounds inflicted on them and are cured? And some birds seek a cure for constipation by drinking sea-water

and are relieved? Such examples are cited in books
of medicine and pharmacy.

You may have doubts about the purpose of plants
growing in deserts where there is no man or beast or
cattle, and think that there is no need for them; but
this is not so, because their purpose is to be fodder for
wild beasts and for birds, their stalks are fuel which
people can use. There are among them, moreover,
some which are medicinal, others which tan animal
hides, still others used for dyeing, and so on.

Do you not see that papyrus and esparto grass and
other such plants are amongst the basest plants?
However, there are many uses for them. Writing
materials can be made from them, which may be
used by kings and commoners; mats, which
everybody uses, packing material to protect utensils,
especially on journeys so that they may not break or
get damaged, and other such uses, things great and
small, valuable or otherwise. Baser still than these
plants are droppings and dung which combine
baseness with pollution. Yet for vegetables and
pulses and other plants they serve a function which
nothing else can serve, to the extent that no type of
vegetable would prosper were it not for droppings
and dung which men consider filthy and hate to
approach. The status of a particular thing in the
world of knowledge does not necessarily accord with

its market value: there are different statuses for
different markets. Something that is base in the
commercial market may be very precious in the
marketplace of knowledge. Do not underestimate the
lesson that may be taught by an object because of its
small market value.

FOUR

Animals

The bodies of animals

Consider the structure of animals' bodies, and how they are constituted in the way they are, neither rigid like stones, unable to bend and unsuitable for doing work, nor so soft and pliable that they are not sturdy enough to keep their shape and identity. They are made of soft, pliable flesh with rigid bones inside for support and muscles and veins to provide tension. Everything is put together and encased in the skin which covers the whole body, like toy animals made of sticks with rags and strings wrapped around them, covered with resin. The sticks act like bones, the rags like flesh, the strings like ligaments and veins, and the resin covering like skin. If you argue that the living, mobile animal happens by accident and without a maker, then these lifeless toys are more likely to be accidents. And even if you argued that these toys appeared by accident, it would be more difficult to argue the same for animals.

Cattle

Think, further, about the bodies of cattle. They are created similar to the bodies of men, from meat, bones and muscle, and are also given hearing and sight so that people can use them for their benefit. If cattle were blind and dumb, people could have no service from them nor could they do what people want. Beyond that, however, animals were denied intellect and mind so that they submit to human control and do not resist when driven hard, and loaded with heavy burdens. You may argue that there are human slaves who are humbled and submit to great fatigue, who nevertheless have not been denied intellect and mind. We would reply that such people are very few. The majority of people do not submit to carrying heavy loads, pulling grinding mills and similar tasks, as animals do. Nor could such people fulfil the tasks animals do. If people were to carry out such physical labour with their own bodies it would take them away from other work: in place of one camel or mule you would need several men. Such work would take all their time, leaving them none for the development of other crafts and professions, to say nothing of the great bodily fatigue and misery they would experience.

Human beings and animals: carnivores and herbivores

Reflect how the following three types of animals were made in a way appropriate to the best interests of each. When it was ordained that human beings would have intellect and intelligence, and the ability to practise building, carpentry, sewing, butchery and such other works, they were given large hands with thick fingers that can grasp things and carry out various crafts. Carnivores, when they were created to live by hunting, were endowed with small,

45

compact paws, with claws and talons suitable for catching prey, but unsuitable for crafts. When it was ordained that herbivores would have no crafts nor catch prey, some were endowed with cloven hooves, tough enough to protect them from the ground as they roam about to graze, some were given single hooves which were concave like feet so that they would rest firmly on the ground and be suitable for loading and riding on.

Reflect on the design in the creation of carnivorous animals. They were created with sharp teeth, strong claws and wide mouths because it was intended that they should feed on meat. They were created in an appropriate way, equipped with weapons and tools suitable for hunting. You find the same with predatory birds which are equipped with beaks and talons appropriate to their function. If wild cattle had claws they would have redundant equipment because they do not hunt or eat meat; and if predatory animals had cloven hooves they would be deprived of the weapons they need to hunt and catch their food. Do you not see how each kind was given what suits its nature and function, and what enables it to live its own proper life?

Look at the young of quadrupeds: how they follow their mothers independently, not needing to be carried or brought up like human offspring. Since

their mothers were not endowed with the capacity
for gentle nurturing, knowledge and training that is
peculiar to human mothers, nor with proper hands
and fingers to do these things, animal young were
given the ability to stand up and be independent.
You find the same true of the young of many birds,
like heath-cocks, chickens and partridges which
move about and peck at things as soon as they
hatch from the egg. As for those which are weak
and unable to stand, like pigeon chicks and lark
chicks, their mothers were given extra tenderness
so that they regurgitate the food which they have
stored in their crops to make it soft and easy for the
chick to eat. Such mothers will continue doing this
until the young bird stands up to lead an
independent life. Each creature was given its proper
share of wise design.

Look at the legs of animals, how they were provided
in pairs so that it would be easy to walk. Had they
only had a single leg, they would be useless, since a
walking animal moves some legs while standing on
others. An animal which has two legs moves one and
stands on the other. A quadruped moves two legs
simultaneously on alternate sides while standing on
the others. If it moved two legs on one side and
stood on two on the other, it would not be able to
keep its balance on the ground, just as an armchair
or similar object cannot stand on two legs on one

side. The chair, it must be noted, has no life while an animal has life which makes it move, so it moves the right front leg with the back left while keeping the other two stationary: it thus keeps its balance and does not fall down when it walks.

Animals' subservience to humans

Think how the donkey submits to being loaded and made to turn grindstones when it can see the horse living in luxury; how the camel submits to being led by a young boy even though, if it rebelled, it would prove stronger than a good number of men; how the powerful ox submits to its owner when he puts the yoke on its neck to plough the land; how the noble horse submits to riders carrying swords and spears – it advances and retreats, and responds to a slight pull of the rein – even if the rider chooses to make it charge against swords, it does so; how a flock of sheep submits to a single shepherd, even though it would be impossible to stop them if they chose to move in different directions; and how other types of animals are subject to human beings. How was this possible, except through their being deprived of mind and reflection? If they were to reflect, they would be more likely to disobey human wishes – the camel would resist its leader, the ox its owner and the sheep the shepherd. Likewise, if the predatory animals had mind and reflection, they would be able to combine and cooperate in assaulting people. Who

could withstand lions, tigers, wolves, hyenas, bears,
insects and snakes if they could unite against man?
Do you not see how they are denied this power to
pose a threat; that with all their savagery and might,
they seem to be afraid of human beings. They fear to
come near human habitations and do not venture
abroad to seek food except at night. They were
designed to keep away from human beings,
otherwise they would have been able to attack them
in their houses and restrict their movements.

Do you not see how the dog, although it is similar to
a predatory animal, climbs on walls and roofs in the
darkness of night to guard its owner's house and
repel intruders? It may love its owner so much that
it will sacrifice itself in defence of his cattle and
property. It may become so devoted to him that it
will patiently bear hunger and thirst with him. Why
is the dog designed to be domesticated and love
humans, if not to guard them and their property in
their absence? Moreover, being designed to guard
humans, he is equipped with teeth and claws and a
loud bark to terrify thieves – suspicious characters
avoid places guarded by dogs. The dog has
unswerving courage, endless patience, speed
enough to catch deer, and a sense of smell which
can pick up the scent of birds and hares and foxes
in their habitats, and so on.

Physiology
The position of the vagina

Think: why is the beast of burden's back made
horizontal and supported on four legs, if not to make
it ready for riding and loading? Why was its vagina
made to protrude from behind, if not to allow the
stallion to copulate? If it were at the bottom of the
belly like that of a woman, the stallion would be
unable to do so. Do you not see that he cannot come
to her face to face as a man comes to a woman?
Aristotle's book on animals states that the vagina of
a she-elephant is in the lower part of her belly; when
the time comes for copulation it rises and presents
itself to the bull-elephant so that he is able to
penetrate. Just think how the elephant's vagina,
made differently from other domestic animals, was
given this characteristic, so as to be ready for the
essential act of procreation.

Fur and hair

See how animals' bodies are clothed with hair and
fur to protect them from cold and harm. Their legs
are given various types of hooves to protect the feet
from being worn away. Since they are beasts that
lack intelligence with no hands or fingers for
spinning and weaving, they are spared injury by
being clothed naturally in a permanent coat which
they do not need to renew or exchange. In contrast,
people have intelligence and hands suitable for

work: they spin and weave and wear clothing, and change it over and over again. All of this is advantageous to them from various points of view: through work they keep themselves away from folly, idleness and its consequences; they derive comfort from taking off their coats and putting them on at will; they also experience joy and pleasure in obtaining all kinds of beautiful clothing at different times; moreover, they get pleasure from being naked at times and dressed at others; and they exercise their craftsmanship in making all kinds of shoes and slippers to protect their feet. Thus, hair and fur function as clothing for animals, and hooves as shoes.

Dying wild animals hide themselves

Reflect on another amazing characteristic of wild animals: they hide their dead as humans do – for where are the corpses of wild beasts and animals? We see none, but there are not so few as to escape notice. It would be correct to say that there are more animal corpses than human. Compare the numbers of animals we observe in deserts: all kinds of gazelles, mountain goats, antelope, deer; the different predatory animals such as lions, hyenas, wolves, tigers and others; varieties of flying and crawling insects; and flocks of birds – crows, sand-grouse, geese, cranes, pigeons and predatory birds. Where do they all go? Why do we not see their remains except for the occasional one caught by a hunter or savaged by a predator? Reason demands that when they feel the approach of death they hide in secret places and die there. Were that not so, the wilderness would be so full of corpses that they would pollute the air and spread diseases and plagues. Reflect on how that practice, which people have arrived at by thought and reflection, was made innate in animals so as to spare men harm. As for those animals, birds and insects which live among human beings, they were not given the instinct we see in wild animals because people are able to move their corpses and make arrangements to prevent any harm arising from them. All these facts indicate that the world did not come about by chance and neglect.

The faces of animals

Reflect on the faces of animals that are ridden. You will observe that the eyes are placed at the front so that they can see ahead of them and do not hit walls or stumble into holes but protect themselves and their riders. You will see that the mouth opens at the bottom of the muzzle so that they can bite fodder. If it were in the front of the muzzle, like a man's mouth and chin, they would not have been able to pick up food from the ground. Do you not admit that man cannot pick up food with his mouth, but must do so with his hand? As these animals have no hands to pick up fodder, their mouths were made to open at the end of their muzzles so that they can put them into the fodder and take mouthfuls, and they were given lips to gather food both near and far so that they lose none of it.

If someone doubts the benefits of the tail we would say, that to the best of our knowledge it has many. First it is like a lid that covers the anus and the vagina to hide them. There is dirt that collects between the anus and the belly, where flies, mosquitoes and ticks collect; the animal uses the tail like a whisk to drive away these pests. Moreover, the animal finds comfort in moving the tail and waving it to right and left because its body is supported on all fours, and the front legs are occupied in carrying the body so that they cannot move freely and turn: the animal finds pleasure and comfort in using the tail. There may be other benefits which we are not aware of, and which some may deride because they notice their usefulness only in times of need: for instance, an animal may slip and fall down in the mud, and nothing is more help in getting it to its feet again than to pull it by the tail.

Elephants' trunks
Consider the elephant's trunk and the subtle design evident in it. It acts like a hand to pick up food and drink and convey it to the stomach. Without it the

elephant would not be able to pick up anything from the ground because it has no neck to stretch like cattle. Thus, since it was denied a neck, it was given instead this long trunk with which to satisfy its needs. It is made hollow because it is a container for conveying food and drink to the stomach. The elephant uses it as an attack weapon and also to give and take. Who gave it something to replace the organ it lacked if not the Creator who is clement to his creatures? How could all this happen by chance as the wicked say?

If you ask, 'Why was it not created with a neck like cattle?' we answer that, as far as we understand, the head, ears and tusks are massive and very heavy. If they were placed on a neck it would weaken and collapse, unable to bear them. Its head was made to be attached directly to its body in order to prevent this; instead, it was given that long trunk to obtain what it needs in spite of lacking a neck. Furthermore, this was so in order that variety in creation would be a stronger indication of the power and design of the Creator. One animal picks up food with its trunk, another uses its neck, and yet another its beak; some beaks bend towards the chest, others bend sideways; one is made broad, one narrow and another like a claw, each appropriate to its way of life, picking up grains or hunting for food. Some animals crawl on their bellies, others walk on two legs and others go on four, all to manifest the power of the Lord of the Universe to create what He wishes, as He pleases, and He has power over everything.

Giraffes

Reflect on the creation of the giraffe and how different and similar its limbs are to the limbs of other animals. Because its head and skin are like that of a leopard, its neck like that of a camel and its hooves like those of cows some have claimed it was produced from different stallions. They say this is caused by different wild animals mounting grazing animals when they come to water thus producing a hybrid, but this theory cannot rationally be sustained because few animals fertilise another species: the horse does not fertilise the camel nor the camel the cow. Fertilisation occurs only between a few kinds of animals and other closely related ones: the horse fertilises the donkey and produces the mule; the wolf fertilises the hyena and produces a lycaon. However, the offspring does not have a distinct organ of each as we observe in the giraffe which has one organ like that of the horse and another like that of the camel; rather it would be somewhere in between, a mixture of both, as you see in the mule. You find its head, rump and hooves somewhere between those of the horse and donkey. Even the sound of its voice is somewhere between the whinny of the horse and the bray of the donkey.

This indicates that the giraffe is not, as has been claimed, a product of varieties of animals; rather it is an amazing creation of God indicating His power which nothing can hinder, and showing that He is the Creator of all varieties of animals. It is His pleasure to place whatever organs He wishes in any animal, and to distinguish the varieties with appropriate organs. The long neck of the giraffe is advantageous to it because, as knowledgeable people say, it grows up and grazes in thickets with very tall trees. The giraffe needs a long neck to cull its food from the tops of such trees.

The monkey and its similarity to humans

Think how similar the monkey's shape is to that of the human being – its head, face, chest, shoulders and even its interior organs – as Aristotle noted in his book on animals, and as other medical books have confirmed. Consider the intelligence and cleverness with which it has been endowed which enable it to understand what its keeper wants it to do. It also responds to training, understands signals and imitates much of what human beings can do. It is even similar to them in its nature and characteristics. It was designed to be like that to teach human beings a lesson that they are made from the same material as animals and are similar to them in features. So close are they to them that they should learn not to be arrogant and rebel against their Creator: were it not for the special quality of intellect and mind with which God has endowed them, they would have been indistinguishable from some animals. On the other hand, there are other things which differentiate a monkey from a human being, the snout for instance, and the triceps, the long tail and the hair that covers the whole body. However, all this would not have stopped the monkey from catching up with the human being, had he been given a similar intellect and intelligence. In fact, the only thing that separates him from human beings, is lack of intellect.

Have you heard what is related about the dragon and the clouds? They say that clouds are given the task of snatching a dragon whenever they see one as a magnet attracts a piece of iron, so that it will not venture its head out of the ground for fear of clouds, and will emerge only rarely, when the sky is clear without a speck of cloud. Why were the clouds given the task of looking out for this animal and snatching it, if it were not to prevent it from harming people? If you object, 'Why was this animal created at all?' we answer, 'To frighten people. It is like a whip to frighten suspicious characters, in order to discipline them and teach them a lesson.'

Animal intelligence and stratagems
Reflect on the kinds of intelligence with which

animals were endowed for their own benefit –
natural instinct, not mind or reflection. A stag, they
say, eats snakes and becomes very thirsty, but
refrains from drinking water for fear of the poison
running into its body and killing it. Although it is so
thirsty, it will stand at a pool roaring loudly, but will
not drink until it knows that the poison has
dispersed and that it has digested its meal. Consider
the patience made innate in this animal and how it
endures great thirst for fear of injury, something
which a rational man rarely does – for all his
intelligence, a man can scarcely control himself! It
is common knowledge that when the fox lacks food it
will pretend that it is dead, and puff up its belly so
that birds will be taken in. When they alight to eat
it, it will leap up and catch them. Who equipped the
fox, which has no mind, speech or reflection, with
this trick, if it were not the One who undertook to
provide for it in this and in many other ways? Since
the fox was less able to overpower game, as larger
hunting animals do, it was enabled to get its own
provision through intelligence and cunning. The
dolphin, they say, tries to catch birds by trickery: it
catches a fish, kills it, and tears it open, and lets it
float on the water while lurking underneath. It
muddies the water so that it is not seen. When birds
swoop down for the floating fish, the dolphin leaps
up and catches them. Consider how this subtle trick
is bestowed innately on this animal for its

advantage. Listen also to what they say about the crocodile: when pieces of meat collect between its teeth and rot, becoming infested with worms which irritate, it goes out on to the shore, and opens its mouth as if it were dead. Birds then come down and pick out the worms. When the crocodile realises that its mouth is clean, it shuts it, so trapping the birds and swallowing them. Hence we have the proverb: 'I will reward you as the crocodile does.'

Moths, ants, fly-lions and spiders
Reflect on the tiny moth. Do you find that it lacks anything that is appropriate for its own kind of life? How did this perfect design come about if not as part of the design we see in both the small and large creatures? You observe these little creatures meeting each other. Two of them will stop, just as a man will stop and shake hands with an acquaintance when he meets him and asks him about his life. Consider how ants gather together to collect food and store it for their hibernation. A group of ants transporting grains to their nest are like a group of people carrying food or something similar. Indeed you find in ants more seriousness and earnest work than you would among human beings! They can be seen cooperating in the work of transport as humans cooperate at work. They cut the grains into pieces to prevent them sprouting and becoming useless to them; if the grains get wet, they will bring them out to dry. They establish their

store on high ground so that it does not flood. They do all this without having mind or reflection, only an inbuilt instinct, with which they are endowed for the sake of their own welfare.

Observe one kind of spider (in Syriac 'fly-lion') and the cunning it has been given in seeking its food. When it senses that a fly has settled nearby it waits for a while, motionless, as if it were dead. When the fly finds no threat in its presence, it crawls very gently to a position from which the spider can catch it in one leap. Then it smothers it with its whole body, fearing that the fly will leap away. It also deliberately pricks the fly's wings and restrains the fly with its own hands and feet to prevent escape; the spider continues to hold it until it feels that it has weakened, until finally it swallows the fly, and this is how it lives. Just as humans weave cloth, other spiders weave webs as a trap for flies and lurk inside them. When the flies are enmeshed, they sting them time after time and suck them dry for food. The first kind resembles hunting with hounds and panthers; the second, hunting with nets and ropes. Just contemplate how this weak animal performs by instinct something which man has been able to achieve only by stratagems and tools. Never disregard what can be learned from moths or ants, and similar small things; great significance can be gleaned from small examples with no loss of validity,

60

even as a golden dinar can be weighed against an iron or stone weight with no loss of value.

The shape of birds' bodies

Reflect on the body and the shape of the bird. Since it was ordained that the bird should fly in the sky, its body was made light and compact. Instead of four legs it was given two; instead of five toes, four, and the two outlets for droppings and urine were combined in one. A bird's shape is streamlined to penetrate the air more easily, just as the front of a ship is so shaped as to cleave the water and force a way through it. In the wings and tail there are placed sturdy feathers so that it can fly. Its whole body is covered with feathers so that the air can pass between them and keep it aloft. Since it was ordained that it should feed on grains and meat, which it swallows without chewing, it was not given teeth but a tough, curved beak instead with which it can peck its food and which cannot be broken by pecking grain or tearing at meat. Since it was not endowed with teeth but was made to swallow the grains and pieces of raw meat whole, it was given greater interior heat to break down the food. Thus it does not need to chew it at length, for you know how grape-seeds and similar foods issue intact from human intestines, whereas they are crushed inside the belly of birds, so that no trace is seen of them when they are excreted.

The chicken and the egg

Birds were also made to lay eggs, rather than
gestating chicks, so that they do not become too
heavy to fly. If the embryo were to develop in the
belly and stay there until it reached sustainable
independent existence, the bird would become too
heavy to leave the ground. Do you not see that
everything is fashioned to suit the way of life for
which it was created? Why were birds of the air
made to sit on their nests and hatch their brood for
a week or two? Some birds will even regurgitate
food after it has settled in their crop, and feed it to
their young. Why does a bird accept such hardship
when it has no power of reflection or forethought,
and cannot hope to benefit from its offspring, as
human beings can take pride in their children, and
hope to enjoy their kindness and support and
eventually have their name kept alive. A bird's
instinctive kindness to its chicks has a reason it is
unaware of, that is, the procreation and continuance
of the species.

Observe how the hen is disposed to brood the eggs
and chicks, even when she has no clutch of eggs or
suitable place for them. She gets excited, puffs
herself up and clucks, denies herself to the cockerel
and stops feeding until the eggs are gathered. She
then broods over them to hatch them. Why should
she do this if not for the sake of procreation? She

has no power of reflection or thought for consequences. Notice the thick, yellow yolk, and the thinner white liquid. One part contains the chick as it grows, while the rest provides food for it until it hatches. Think of the design in all this: since it was planned that the chick would grow inside this hard, impenetrable shell, sufficient food was provided inside to last until it hatches, just like someone imprisoned in a fortified tower with nothing reaching him, yet provided with sufficient food until his release.

Crop, feathers, legs and necks of birds
Think of the purpose for which the crop of a bird is designed. The path of the food to the gizzard is very narrow and can only admit a tiny amount at a time. If the bird waited to peck a second grain until after the first had reached the gizzard, feeding would take a long time. Since great caution leads it to feed stealthily, how could it collect enough food? The crop was therefore provided like a nosebag in front of the bird so that it can store food quickly, but the food reaches the gizzard slowly. There is another use for the crop. Some birds must feed their young and it is easier to regurgitate food from a nearer container.

How could the diversities of colour and pattern in birds' plumage happen as a result of mixing the different humours haphazardly. And does the ornamentation we find in the peacock, pheasant and francolin come about be chance? The straight and criss-cross lines look as if they are drawn with a pen; how could this uniformity be haphazard? Consider a bird's feather and how it is made. You will notice that it is woven like a garment of fine fibres brought close to each other, as thread to thread and hair to hair. If you spread this weaving, it will open slightly without tearing, so that the air will permeate it and support the bird in flight. The axis of the feather is a thick, stiff stem, to which a hair-like web is firmly attached. This shaft along the middle of the feather is hollow so that it is light and does not hinder the bird in flight.

Have you observed the long-legged heron and discovered what benefits it derives from the length of its legs? Normally it feeds in shallow water, perched on these two legs as if on a watch-tower, to observe what moves beneath it. When a desirable morsel comes along, it steps stealthily towards it and spears it. Had the heron been constructed with short legs, its belly would agitate the water and the frightened prey would escape. Thus it was created with those long stilts in order to get its sustenance without undue difficulty.

Think of another example of good design in the creation of birds. You will observe that every long-legged bird is long-necked so that it can reach its food on the ground. If it were short-necked and long-legged it would not be able to peck anything on the ground. Feeding may further be facilitated and made more effective not only by the long neck but also by the length of the beak. Do you not see that whenever you inspect the Creation carefully you find that it was made with the utmost appropriateness and wisdom?

Sparrows and bats

Consider how sparrows seek their food throughout the day, neither going without it nor finding it already gathered; they obtain it by searching. You will observe that the same is true of all provender. Glory be to Him who measured it out, separated it, dispersed it, without making it impossible to obtain. He created His creatures' need for it but did not make it readily available or easily obtainable, since this was not in their best interest. If it were already collected, animals would keep on eating it, until they overfed and perished; and if there were only great abundance and leisure people would have fallen into the utmost indolence, so that there would be great corruption and depravity.

Can you identify the food of night-flying creatures, like owls and bats? It is said that they feed airborne on moths, butterflies, crickets, drones and so on,

since such creatures are present in the air in such
great numbers that nowhere is free of them. If you
place a lamp in the yard of a house at night all kinds
of insects will come to it. Where do they come from
if they are not nearby? If anyone should say they
come from the deserts and open spaces, we ask how
they could come from such great distances, attracted
by a lamp in a house surrounded by other houses?
We also note that they fall on the lamp from all
sides, an indication that the air is thick with them.
The flying creatures we have mentioned come out to
seek and feed on them. Reflect how provision from
these insects spread about in the air was sent to
those flying creatures which come out only at night.
You should also note the significance of God
creating these types of insects which some might
think have no use at all.

The bat is created in an amazing way – it is a cross
between a bird and a four-legged animal. Indeed it
is closer to a four-legged animal in that it has two
erect ears and also has teeth and fur. Its
characteristics are different from those of birds in
that it menstruates, becomes pregnant, produces
young, suckles them, urinates and walks on all
fours. It is also nocturnal and feeds on the insects
present in the air and other such food. Some say that
moths do not feed at all, and others that bats feed
only on air, but these assertions can be denied on

two counts: first, bats excrete droppings and urine, and these can only derive from food; second, they have teeth: there would be no sense in their having teeth if they did not feed. There is nothing without a purpose in Creation. The benefits to be gained from bats are described in medical texts, their droppings are even used in some *kohls*. One of the best things is that their wonderful nature proves how the great power of the Creator is manifest in everything He wills, demonstrating all kinds of benefits.

A trustworthy man has related that a small bird, a *sylvia*, made its nest in a tree and on one occasion he observed a huge snake crawling towards it, hissing, its mouth wide open to swallow it. While the bird was jumping about in panic, seeking a stratagem for escape, it found a thorn which it took and threw into the mouth of the snake. The snake began to writhe in pain until it died. Now, if we had not been told this story, could it be imagined that a small thorn could be so useful? Many things contain a value that is discovered only in particular circumstances, after which the matter becomes common knowledge.

Bees and locusts
Consider how bees congregate to make honey and prepare hexagonal cells adapted to their needs. Their very subtle instincts have been described by

naturalists. If you observe their work you will find it amazingly skilful. If you evaluate the product you will find it full of noble significance for mankind; if you look at the workers they are stupid and ignorant, unaware of themselves, let alone of others. Here is the clearest evidence that the perfect adaptation of the work of bees to its purpose comes not from the bees themselves, but from Him who created them in this way, and subjected them to human beings in their labour, to humanity's great advantage.

Think how weak locusts are and yet how powerful are their effects. You must admit that, although the locust is one of the weakest of creatures, no one can protect a town from advancing armies of them. If a mighty king were to gather all his horses and men to protect a town from locusts he would not be able to do so. Is this not evidence of the power of the Creator who can pit His weakest creature against His mightiest, who cannot repel it. See how locusts advance across the face of the earth like a flood, covering valley and mountain, bedouin and urban areas, till they hide the light of the sun in their multitudes. If they were made by human hands, how long would it take to gather such vast numbers? And how many years would it be before they could fly? Learn from this one sign of the Power which nothing can overwhelm or outdo.

Fish

Consider how well-suited the structure of the fish is to the way it was intended to live; since it lives in water and does not need to walk, it has no legs. Since it cannot breathe while submerged in the depths of the sea, it is created without lungs. Instead of legs, it is given strong fins, with which it propels itself like a boatman with side-mounted oars. Its body is covered with tough scales, interwoven like armour or a coat of mail, to protect it from predators. It is aided with a more acute sense of smell because its sight is poor and the water impedes vision. Fish can smell their prey from a long distance and seek it out, otherwise how could they locate it? Aristotle states that there are tubes between the mouth and the ears; by swallowing water through its mouth and passing it through to the ears, the fish gets the same sensation as animals which breathe air.

Reflect on the characteristic prodigality of fish spawn. Countless eggs develop in the belly of a single fish. The explanation for this is that in this way there is enough for all sorts of animals that feed on fish. Most animals – even beasts of prey – eat fish; they can be found at the edge of the forest crouching over clear water waiting for fish, and when one passes by it will be caught. Since beasts of prey, birds, mankind, and also fish all eat fish, and there are other creatures in the sea which feed

on nothing but fish, it is wise that they should be
so numerous.

If you want to understand how great is the wisdom of
the Creator, and how small the knowledge of
creatures, observe the countless varieties of fish,
shellfish and other sea creatures, whose uses can be
discovered only gradually and by accident. They say
that crimson dye was discovered when a bitch found
some sea snails on the beach at Tyre and ate them.
Her muzzle was smeared with their blood. People
saw that it was attractive and began to use it as a
dye for silk. There are many other such things which
people discover from time to time.

FIVE

Human Beings

From the womb to puberty

I now turn to the creation of mankind, and the evidence there of Divine wisdom, design and execution. First is the design of the support system for the foetus in the womb: at a time when it cannot seek food or protect itself from harm, blood from its mother feeds it as water feeds a plant. When its development is complete, its body grown strong, its skin fit to encounter the air and its eyes the light, contractions will occur, so greatly disturbing and agitating the foetus that it is born. After birth the food-bearing blood of its mother will be transferred to her breasts and transformed into another form of food more suitable for the newly born. So the milk comes to it as needed. When the child is born its lips are ready to suckle and will find two breasts like small skin flasks, hanging there to satisfy its need. The infant continues to feed on milk as long as its body is soft and its intestines feeble; but when it becomes more mobile and needs solid nourishment to strengthen its bones and flesh, its teeth will grow, enabling the child to chew food, making it soft and easy to swallow. Further development occurs when the child reaches puberty. If the child is male, hair will grow on his chin – a glorious sign of his masculinity – as he leaves the stage of childhood and similarity to women. If the child is female, her face remains free of hair so that its freshness and lustre remain, which moves men to ensure the continuation of the species.

Think, now, about the structure of human beings, and the design which makes them pass through these various stages. Can any of this be the result of chance? Just think: if blood did not flow to the foetus in the womb, would it not wither and dry up like a plant without water. If it were not disturbed by contractions when it reaches full term, would it not remain in the womb, like a female child buried in the ground at birth? If milk were denied it at birth, would it not die of hunger or feed on something unsuitable for and harmful to its body. If teeth did not emerge in time, it would not be able to chew food and would have to persist in suckling, so that its body would not become strong or suitable for work. It would keep its mother occupied and not free to look after another child. If hair did not eventually grow on a man's face, would he not continue to look like a child or woman, without the dignity of an impressive appearance? Who could see to bringing about all these necessary developments in due time other than the One who created human beings out of nothing, and undertook to supply them with all that is good for them? If chance could explain all this magnificent design, we would have to say that plan and design come about by accident and without thought which would be absurd.

Mental development

Look at human beings another way: at birth they
are without understanding, ignorant, unaware. If
they were born with awareness and understanding
they would be utterly bewildered as they saw things
they did not recognise and discovered things they
had not seen before. Compare this with a boy taken
as a captive to a strange country after he has
developed awareness and understanding. He is
bewildered and perplexed, and will not learn the
language and accept training like a child growing
up within its own environment. Similarly, if a child
were born with awareness of himself, he would
object to seeing himself carried, suckled and
swaddled in cloths and made to lie in the cradle,
although he cannot survive without all this,
because his body is soft and tender at birth. We
would not feel the same tenderness of heart for him
nor would we experience the compassion and joy
that is our normal response to a child. As it is, an
infant enters the world ignorant and unaware of
what people are about. He takes things in with a
small intellect and a little knowledge which
increases gradually as time goes by until he is used
to things and trained to handle them. He moves
from the stage of gazing in bewilderment to that of
conducting his own affairs and getting involved in
daily life.

Furthermore, if he were born with complete understanding and fully independent there would be no place for bringing up children, nor would we have the benefit accruing from parents bringing up their children, and the duty entailed on the child to reward his parents with goodness and kindness when they need it. Nor would children have become familiar with their parents and the parents with their children, since children would need no care or education from their parents, and would disperse at birth with the result that a man would not know his father or his mother nor would they know him. He would not refrain from copulation with his mother or his sister, since he would not know either of them. The very least that would happen is that the child would come out of his mother's belly fully aware, and see parts of her body which are neither lawful nor proper for him to see!

Is it not clear that everything in Creation is perfectly made, and that whatever is inappropriate – large or small – is avoided? Medical and physiological books tell us that a foetus is made from the fluids of the male and female in conjunction. The male injects his fluid into the woman's uterus and the woman releases her fluid within her own uterus, nowhere else. There they mix and from them the foetus results, by the will and power of God.

Reproductive organs
See how aptly are constructed the organs of
intercourse in male and female for their purpose.
Since the male needs to inject his fluid into
another creature, he was endowed with a
projecting instrument which can extend so that it
makes the sperm reach the uterus. The female, on
the other hand, who needs to contain the two fluids
together and bear the foetus until it is fully
developed, was endowed with a hollow receptacle
suitable for that purpose.

Parts of the body
Think how each part of the body is designed to suit
its purpose: the hands for handling, the legs for
walking, the eyes for guidance, the ears for hearing,
the nose for smelling, the mouth for feeding, the
stomach for digesting, the liver for purification, the
outlets for excretion, the tubes for conveying
substances, and the genitals for maintaining
reproduction. Similarly, if you reflect on all other
parts you will find each of them designed to the
highest standards of wise appropriateness.

If you claim that all this was done by Nature, we
would ask you about this 'Nature'. Is it something
which has knowledge and power to do all these
things or not? If you accept that it has knowledge
and power, what prevents you from accepting the

existence of the Creator since these are the
characteristics of the Creator? If, on the other hand,
you claim that Nature does all these things without
knowledge and intention, this is absurd, since you
can see all this wise appropriateness around you. It
could not have arisen without knowledge and
intention. It thus becomes clear that this is the doing
of the Great Creator, and what you had named
'Nature' is nothing but the way of this Creator.

How nourishment gets to the body

Reflect on the design in the way nourishment
reaches the body. Food enters the stomach which
reduces it to a pulp. This is then sent to the liver
through the very narrow tubes connecting them.
These act like strainers, so that nothing rough or
large may reach the liver and injure it, since it is
delicate and cannot tolerate harsh treatment. The
liver then turns the pulp into blood which it sends
to the whole body in purpose-built veins, like
canals that carry water to all parts of the land. The
waste and filth are then sent to containers prepared
for them. Bile-like matter goes to the gall bladder
attached to the liver, black bile to the spleen, fluid
to the bladder.

The structure of the body

Reflect on the wise design evident in the structure
of the body: in the location of these organs and the

construction of channels to carry the waste away so that it may not permeate the body and harm it. If you wished to enlarge a small figure made of alum, copper or wax, could you do so without breaking and remoulding it afresh, starting from the head? Consider then how a child's body grows, in all its members, while remaining constant in essence, form and shape. Even more amazing is the way it develops in the womb, where no eye can see and no hand can reach, yet the baby comes out well shaped and complete with all the components it needs for its welfare – stomach, limbs, and body fluids, in addition to its truly wisely designed and very finely structured bones, flesh, fat, marrow, muscles, veins and cartilage.

Consider what distinguishes human beings from the rest of God's Creation: how they are honoured and placed above animals. They are created to stand erect and sit upright, to hold things with their hands and limbs, and to manipulate and work on them. If they were made horizontal, like four-legged animals, they would not be able to do any such work. For this reason, the word for a human being in Greek is derived from 'contemplating higher things', according to Plato, or from 'looking upwards' according to other authorities.

The senses and deprivation of them

Note how the organs of vision, by means of which
our souls perceive things, were placed in the head
like lamps at the top of a lighthouse. They were not
put into the working limbs such as hands and legs,
and thereby exposed to injury from work and
movement, nor were they placed in the middle of the
body, like the belly or the back from which it would
be difficult to see over things. Such locations would
be inappropriate and the head is the most suitable
place for them.

Some philosophers have rightly described the head
as being the storehouse of the senses. Who made the
senses five, other than Him who made perceivable
things in five categories. He planned five senses
that perceive five sensations so that nothing
perceivable would be missed. If you say, 'Perhaps
there are sensations which we have no senses to
perceive?' We would say, 'It is impossible that there
are perceivable things that are not perceived by the
senses, because they would be redundant and
meaningless, and there is nothing meaningless in
creation: all sages and philosophers have concluded
this and our experience testifies to it, too.' Why was
the sight created, if not to perceive colours, shapes
and light? Why was hearing created if not to
perceive sounds? If there were colours without sight,
sounds without hearing, what use would they be? –

and so on with the rest of the senses. Conversely, if we had sight without colour, hearing without sounds, what would be the meaning of sight and hearing? Reflect how they were made appropriate to each other, each sense having its own sensation, and each sensation having its own sense.

Reflect also on realities like light and air, which were established as a necessary medium between senses and sensations. Without light, colour could not be perceived by the sight; without air to carry sound, hearing could not detect it. Is there any sensible person who cannot admit that this matching of senses and objects, appropriate to each other in conception and construction, could not have come about without intention and design? Think of a sightless person, and the trouble that afflicts his whole life. He cannot see where to put his foot or what is in front of him. He cannot distinguish colours, or beautiful from ugly sights. He receives no warning of a pit he might fall into, or an enemy he could avoid. He does not know whether a sword is raised over him, nor can he undertake such craftsmanship as carpentry, writing or metalwork – so much so, indeed, that if his mind did not remain intact, he would be cast aside like a stone. Similarly, the life of a person who has been deprived of hearing may become deficient in many ways. He lacks the sense of conversation and dialogue and the joy of sounds, of pleasant and touching melodies. He causes people so much trouble that they may resent him, nor does he hear news about people or their conversation: he is like someone absent though present and dead though alive. As for a person who lacks mental faculties, he is relegated to the status of beasts; indeed he is ignorant of things that beasts know. Do you not see that the senses, intellect and other faculties make man's life complete and that if he lacks any of them great deprivation befalls him, even though he is otherwise created fully equipped, lacking nothing? How could this be so, unless the Creation entailed intention and planning?

In short, if it is established that the Maker (Praise be to Him!) is wise and just, He is cleared from any blame for what He has done. He knows best where the best interests and welfare of man lie and what is the future of all his affairs. He (Exalted be He above any comparison!) is like a physician, who is trusted not to err in treating a patient. His remedies might cause discomfort and pain, but this would not be attributed to cruelty or injustice, or error causing harm to the patient. You may ask, 'Why is it that some people suffer the loss of some of their faculties?' We reply, 'This teaches discipline to them and others,' just as nobody considers it bad that a king may discipline some with punishments which are lessons to others; indeed it is accepted and considered prudent. Besides, those who suffer afflictions have rewards in the Hereafter, if they bear them patiently and thank their Lord and turn towards Him. These rewards are so great as to make them regard the affliction as something small – so small that, if they were given the choice after resurrection, they would choose to be returned to such suffering in order to have their rewards increased.

One head; two hands

Think how appropriate and sensible it is that some parts of the body have been created singly and others in pairs. It would not have been an improvement if there were more than one head. If another head were added, it would be unnecessarily heavy on the body, since all the senses that man needs are contained in one head. Had he two heads, his tongue would be divided into two parts, one for each head: if he spoke with one, the other would be idle and useless; if he said the same thing with both of them, one would be redundant; if he said one thing with the first tongue and another with the second, the listener would be confused, and would not know which to listen to. The hands are made in pairs. It would not be good for man to have only one hand, as this would impair his handling of things. Consider a carpenter or a builder: if either of his hands were paralysed he could not practise his profession. Even if he tried, he would not attain the same standard of perfection as with two hands working together.

The voice and speech: versatile organs

Consider how the vocal organs are made; how speech is constructed, with the sounds of the letters made at their places of articulation, using the air provided. Every organ is created for its own particular function. Think how elements of sound are combined into speech: the larynx is like a tube through which the sound issues; the tongue, the lips and the teeth are made to form consonants and vowels. Do you not notice that someone who loses teeth is unable to perfect the sound 's'; someone whose lip is injured cannot pronounce the 'f', and that one whose tongue is heavy cannot pronounce the 'r' properly? How excellently people in earlier times have compared the voice-box with the large bagpipe! They likened the larynx to the chanter and the lung to the bag which squeezes the wind through it. They likened the muscles that contract the lung, producing the sound from the larynx, to hands which squeeze the bag to send the air through the reed pipe; the lips and teeth, which shape sound into letters and intonation, they likened to fingers which play on the holes of the pipe to create the different notes. Although the sound of the voice may be compared to that of the bagpipe it is, in fact, the pipe that should be compared to the human organs of voice production; the bagpipe is artificial and the human voice is natural, and art imitates Nature. However, since artefacts are easier to see and better known to the general public than Nature, the functioning of Nature is compared to that of artefacts to make it easier to understand.

We have explained how useful these organs are in producing speech and in the proper pronunciation of alphabetical sounds. However, they also have other functions. By way of the larynx the air flows to the lungs and refreshes the heart with regular breathing; the tongue makes it possible to taste and recognise foods and distinguish between them, as well as helping to swallow food and drink easily. The teeth chew food to make it tender and easy to swallow. Teeth also function as a support for the lips, to retain and buttress them from inside the mouth; consider how sunken and restless are the lips of a toothless person. Using the lips one can sip liquid, so that it is consumed in the intended quantity, not so much as would choke a person and damage his internal organs. Moreover, the lips are like a door or lid for the mouth which can be opened and closed at will as well as giving the mouth a pleasing appearance; have you not noticed how ugly a person becomes if their lips have been cut off?

All that we have said shows how each of these organs has a special use and that one organ may perform diverse functions. Just as an axe can be used for carpentry, digging, fighting or other types of work, lips are suitable for kissing, sipping water, articulating certain sounds, taking in and blowing out air, and other things.

The brain: protection and cushioning of sensitive organs

When the brain is exposed, have you not noticed how it is wrapped in layers, one on top of another, to protect it from any mishap, and keep it stable? The skull is placed over it like a helmet to protect it from the sharpness of a blow, or a knock on the head. The skull is also adorned with skin and hair, like fur on the head to protect it from excessive heat or cold. Who provided such protection for the brain and planned its character, if not the One who created it, knowing it to be the source of sensation, deserving all such precautions because of its position in the body as seat of the mind?

The purposes of human faculties and organs

Who made the eyelids as covers, the eye-sockets as hollows into which the eyes are inserted, then shaded them with the forehead and eyebrows? Who concealed the heart within the chest cavity, and covered it with a protective armour which conceals it – a fortress of ribs, flesh and muscles, a lightweight, defensive container – and made it a master over the limbs and the senses, the functions of which it controls? Indeed, who made it the residence of the essential human spirit? Who constructed two tubes in the throat, one for sound – the tube leading to the lungs – and the other for food – the oesophagus – leading to the stomach? Who put a lid on the throat to prevent food from reaching the lungs and choking them? Who made the lung an unceasing and unfailing ventilator for the heart so that destructive heat would not be concentrated in it?

Who designed orifices as outlets for urine and faeces, orifices that contract and control excreta so that they do not flow continuously and spoil man's life? How many similar things can one count? Indeed, those we cannot count far exceed even those we can. Why was the stomach made muscular and strong, unless it was intended to digest rough food? Why was the liver made delicate and smooth, unless it was intended to absorb the soft essences of food – a task which is more delicate than that of the stomach?

Why is the delicate marrow ensconced within the hollows of bones, if not to contain and protect it? Why is the flowing blood confined within veins like

water in pipes, if not to control it so that it does not
run dry? Why are nails created at the tips of fingers
and toes if not to protect them and support them in
their work? Why is the inside of the ear twisted like
a helix, if not for sound to travel through to reach the
hearing centre? Others have pointed out, too, that
the spiral blunts the sharpness of the wind, so that it
does not damage the inside of the ears. Why does
man carry generous flesh on his buttocks, if not to
protect him from the ground so that he does not
suffer pain when he sits? Someone whose body is
wasted and whose flesh has withered suffers if
something is not put between him and the ground.

Who made human beings male and female, other
than He who created them to be reproductive? Who
made them reproductive other than He who made
them mortal? Who endowed them with tools of work
other than He who created them to work? Who
created them to work other than He who made them
needy? Who inflicted need on them, other than He
who undertook to reform them? Who chose to endow
only them with reason, other than He who ordained
that they should be judged? Who gave them skills
other than He who gave them possessions? Who
gave them possessions, other than He who will
question them about their possessions? Who
provides them with all that their skills cannot
achieve, other than He to whom sufficient gratitude

cannot be shown. Glorious and Exalted is He, His bounties are numberless.

In his discussion of the design in the Creation of human beings, Aristotle said that there are holes in the heart which fit up against holes in the lung, to take air from the lungs to ventilate the heart. If the holes were not aligned, or were separated from each other, the air could not reach the heart, and this would be fatal. Can anyone who has reason and intelligence entertain the claim that such an arrangement can happen by itself? Do they not see in their very own heart a proof that should prevent them from making such a claim? If you see a door with a catch on one side, do you imagine that it serves no useful purpose, or do you deduce that it fits the latch on the other side, so that both come together to perform a useful function? A male animal, too, is one of a pair: he has a reproductive organ intended to fit the female organ. They come together to bring about the procreation and continuation of the species. May Epicurus perish and be lost, and anyone else like him, if their hearts are so blinded to this amazing Creation that they deny any design or intention in it. If a man's penis were limp all the time, how could it reach the end of the vagina to insert the seed? If it were erect all the time, how could a man turn over in bed or walk about in public with that thing protruding in front of

him? In addition to its ugly appearance, it would
continually stir the passions of all men and women
which would lead them all to copulate, an activity
that would eventually lead to their ruin. Therefore
the penis was designed to be limp most of the time
so that it would not always be visible and would not
cause the male much trouble, but was also endowed
with the ability to stiffen as required, with the
objective of procreation and the continuation of the
species. Is it not a sign of excellent architecture that
the lavatory is placed in the most secluded part of
the house? In the same way you find the outlet for
faeces is placed in the most secluded part of the
human body: it is not protruding behind or
projecting in front, but hidden in a secret part of
the body where fleshy buttocks meet which
conceal it. When the need comes to defecate and
man sits down that in that particular position you
will find that the rectum is pointing down ready
for the faeces to drop.

Teeth, hair and nails
Reflect on the way the grinding teeth (molars) have
been created for man: the incisors are sharp so as to
cut and tear food; the molars are broad so as to
crush and chew. Neither kind is lacking, since there
is need for both. Consider Divine design in the
creation of hair and nails. Since they were made to
grow to such a length that it is necessary to trim

them occasionally, they were made without feeling
so that man does not feel the pain of cutting them. If
cutting the hair or paring the nails involved the
sensation of pain, man would have two distasteful
options: either to leave them to grow long until they
broke off – a heavy burden indeed – or to try and
trim them with all the pain involved. If hair grew
inside the eye, would it not blind it? If it grew inside
the mouth, would it not spoil food and drink? If it
grew on the palm of the hand, would it not impair
feeling, and the tasks which hands perform, such as
greeting? If hair grew in a woman's vagina or on a
man's penis, would it not spoil the pleasure of
coition? Consider how these parts are denied hair
for good reasons and how other parts, where hair is
an adornment, are covered with it. This does not
only apply to man, but to beasts as well. You will
notice the parts mentioned above are likewise free
from hair, and for the same reasons. Do you not
realise how Creation avoids what is inappropriate
and harmful and instead executes what is
appropriate and useful. When the Manichaeans (and
people of similar persuasion) tried to find fault with
nature, they criticised the hair that grows on the
knees, under the armpits, on the thighs and in the
pubic region, but this hair grows in the moisture
which nature sends to these parts, like weeds grow in
a swamp. Do you not see that such parts are more
hidden and more suitable for this excess than other

parts of the body? Such an arrangement places on human beings a wholesome responsibility for the needs of the body: taking care of the body, cleaning it and removing the hair and dirt that covers it reduces wickedness by restraining aggression and distracting people from the consequences of idleness.

Saliva

Consider the benefits of saliva. It was made to run continuously to the mouth to moisten throat and uvula so that they would not become dry. Were they to become dry, people would perish: they could not swallow food without moisture in the mouth to lubricate it. As Hippocrates said: 'Moisture is the steed of food.' Fluids such as bile go to more remote parts of the body where they probably serve natural functions.

The crying of infants

Did you know that crying is good for babies? Physicians say that there is fluid in their heads which if it remained there would have serious consequences. Crying causes this fluid to flow from their heads and this is healthy for their bodies. Is it not possible that a child could benefit from crying without you knowing it? In many other things likewise there may be benefits of which you are ignorant. So do not judge something to be useless just because you do not know its uses: much that

you do not know is known to others, and much that
the knowledge of created beings does not
comprehend is well-known to the Creator – Glory
be to Him!

Fancy has taken aimless flight and said: 'If man's
internal organs had inspection hatches as
underground water channels do, then the physician
would have been able to open them and look inside
to see what was wrong, and insert his hand to
manipulate what he wished to treat. Surely that
would have been better than concealing the interior
parts completely from sight and hand, so that a
physician can diagnose internal disorders only from
ambiguous indicators like the urine, or by means of
probes and similar devices which often involve error
and conjecture which can lead to death.' If access
were so easy, the first consequence would be that
humanity would be free from fear of illness and
death, with such a sense of permanence and health
as would engender presumption, arrogance and
hard-heartedness, as we have mentioned many times
before. Moreover, abdominal fluids would filter out
and leak, soiling the places where people sit and
sleep, as well as their clothes and adornment.
Indeed, it would spoil life itself. Furthermore, the
stomach, the liver and the heart perform their
functions by using the natural heat which is
confined inside the body. If the abdomen had

openings, through which the eye could see and the hand could reach, the cold air would penetrate inside, the natural heat would dissipate and the belly cease to function and so cause death. Do you not see that everything imagination can conceive, that is different from what Creation has provided, is wrong and foolish?

Natural human instincts: feeding, sleeping and coition

Consider those inborn instincts created as part of human nature, which drive people to eat, sleep and have sexual intercourse. Consider the providential wisdom evident in these activities, to each of which there corresponds an innate drive, calling and urging people to perform them. Hunger demands nourishment to keep the body alive and functioning; drowsiness induces sleep to rest and refresh the energies; desire leads to coition which maintains reproduction. If people were not driven by instinct to eat, but only did so because they knew that their bodies needed it, they would be more likely to fail to eat through being busy or lazy and their bodies would disintegrate and perish. Such neglect would be like someone failing to take medicine, treatment or other remedies to cure his body, to the detriment of health and life. Likewise, if people were to go to sleep only when they judge that their bodies need to rest and restore energy they probably would not do so, and this would lead to exhaustion. And if they were moved to coition solely by desire for offspring, it is not unlikely that they would have become lazy about it, so that offspring would decrease or cease altogether, for some people have no desire for, and no interest in reproducing.

Consumption and related functions

You must appreciate how each of these activities, which support human beings and ensure their well-being, are reinforced with a natural drive that prompts and urges action. Physicians have described in medical books the functions of four powers in the body. The first is attraction, which collects food and conveys it to the stomach; the second is retention, which retains food in the body until it is dealt with; the third is digestion, which absorbs food in the stomach, extracts nourishment and distributes it to the body; and the fourth is excretion, which expels residue after the digestive process has removed the nutrients. Note the wise and providential design of these powers, their purpose and necessity. Were it not for attraction, how could people move and seek the food which sustains their body? Were it not for the ability to retain food, how could it stay inside the body until the stomach digests it? Were it not for digestion, how could food be processed so that its nutrients are extracted to nourish the body and satisfy its needs?

And were it not for excretion, how could the residue gradually be expelled from the body?

Do you not realise that these powers were commissioned to do what is good for the body? The body can be compared to a king's palace, in which he has an entourage and household managers: one to determine and supply the needs of the entourage, another to receive and store what comes in until it is to be processed and made ready; the third to process, prepare and distribute supplies amongst the entourage; and a fourth to clean up and dispose of whatever filth and dirt there is in the palace. The king, in this example, is the all-knowing Creator, the Lord of all, the palace is the body, the entourage the limbs and the managers the four powers.

You may opine that since these powers and their functions are described in medical books, it is mere redundant repetition of commonplaces to discuss them here, but we treat them from a different angle from that of medicine. Our approach is different. There, they were dealt with from the point of view of medicine and the physical health; but here they are considered from the point of view of the validity of religious attitudes and the healing of the soul. Correction of religious attitudes can be done in the way we have described, by showing the design and wisdom evident in these powers.

Mental faculties

Consider the place of mental faculties in human life:
I mean thought, imagination, reason, memory and so
on. Only consider, if man were to lose just one of
these – the faculty of memory – what a state he
would be in and what damage would accrue to all
his affairs. He would not remember what wealth he
had, what he owed, what he had taken or given away,
what he had seen or heard, what he had said and
what had been said to him. He would not remember
who had done him favours or harm, what benefited
or harmed him. He would not recognise a road, even
after travelling down it countless times, or have
knowledge even of something he had studied all his
life. He would not benefit from any experience or
draw analogies between present and past events.
Such a person would surely cease to be a human
being and become a beast.

The ability to remember and to forget

Consider how valuable each one of God's bounties is
to human beings, let alone all of them together. The
ability to forget is even more remarkable than the
ability to remember. Unless they could forget,
people could never console themselves in adversity
nor would their grief subside or their resentment
die. They would be able to enjoy nothing in this
world while they remembered their misfortune. They
could not hope that the authorities would forget

about them nor that an envier would cease to envy
them. Just think how memory and forgetfulness,
two opposite faculties, have been implanted in
human beings, each benefiting them in its own
way. What can those who attribute phenomena to
two opposite creators say about the fact that these
opposites combine in a way that is good and
beneficial to man?

Sense of propriety

Think how important and significant is one moral
quality by which man is distinguished from all the
animals – I mean the sense of propriety. Without it,
no guest would be entertained, no promises kept, no
needs satisfied, no good deeds done, no evil deeds
avoided. Many deeds could be brought to mind
which are done out of this sense of propriety. There
are some people who would not observe the rights of
their parents, or return anything entrusted to them,
or abstain from indecency if it were not for this
sense of propriety. Can you not admit that man has
been endowed with all these characteristics for his
own good, and the good of all his affairs?

The ability to speak and write

Think of God's blessing in giving human beings the
faculty of speech, through which they express
themselves and understand the communications of
others. Without it they would have been like animals

which can neither give information about themselves
nor understand information given by another.
Similarly, the ability to write, through which we can
record knowledge about our ancestors for the benefit
of our contemporaries; knowledge of our
contemporaries for the benefit of future generations;
all sciences and branches of knowledge and
literature; dealings done and calculations made.
Were it not for writing, information about whole
generations would be lost; knowledge would be
obliterated; literature would be lost; there would be
great disruption to people's dealings and the entire
order of the world.

You may object that writing and speech are
activities which human beings can devise by their
own ingenuity and intelligence, not something
innate in man. They are skills which people learn by
social interaction and for that reason they differ from
one nation to another: the language and writing of
one nation are different from those of another. Truly
natural gifts, you may say, do not differ from one
person to another. In answer to this I say that,
although man is ingenious in his activities, he
receives the innate capacity for ingenuity as a gift
from God. If he had no intelligence to learn or
tongue suited to speech he could never utter a
word; if he had no hand or fingers capable of
writing, he would never write a thing. This is clear

by making a comparison with animals, which have
no speech or writing.

What humans know

Consider both the knowledge given to human beings
and that withheld from them. They have been
granted all that is appropriate to their religion and
life. That part of knowledge which improves religion
is knowledge of the Creator together with the proofs,
indications and signs which exist in Creation;
further knowledge of what is socially obligatory is
given in order to deal justly with people and to be
good to parents, to fulfil trusts, to share with friends
and needy people, and many other such things,
knowledge and acknowledgement of which may be
found in the nature of people from every nation.
Similarly, human beings have been given knowledge
of what is useful for their worldly life, such as
agriculture, plantation, keeping sheep and cattle,
drawing water, medicines that cure various illnesses,
mines from which varieties of jewels can be
extracted, sailing in ships; diving in the sea; all sorts
of tricks to catch beasts, birds and fish; craft skills;
all kinds of trades and livelihoods, and many other
things which are useful for their life in this world.
They have been given knowledge of all the above to
perfect their religious and worldly life and denied
knowledge of other things which do not concern
them, and which by their very nature they cannot

know. For instance: knowledge of the Unseen and the future and some of the past; of things above the sky, under the earth, in the depths of oceans and different regions of the world; what is in the hearts and minds of men, the contents of the womb, and other such things, the knowledge of which is kept hidden from human beings. When people claim knowledge of such things, such claims are falsified by their obvious errors in prediction and fact. Consider, then, how good it is for people that they have been given the knowledge of all that is necessary for their religion and worldly life, but denied other knowledge so that they may know their status and imperfection.

What has been concealed from them
One of the things concealed from human beings is the duration of their lives. If someone knew his life-span to be short, he would never enjoy life while anticipating his death. He would be like someone whose fortune is nearing exhaustion, fearfully awaiting poverty. The anxiety that afflicts a person at the prospect of losing his life is worse than that of losing his money since, if he loses his money he can derive comfort from the hope that he may regain some of it, but when he is certain that his life is ending, despair will seize him. If, on the other hand, a person were certain of leading a long life, he would indulge in pleasure and wrongdoing,

calculating that he could do this for as long as he liked, and then repent at the end of his life. God will not accept such an attitude. Compare the case of a slave who sets out to annoy his master for a whole year and please him for one day or month. His master would certainly not condone this behaviour, and would not consider that slave a good one unless he had the heartfelt and sincere intention to obey at all times and in all circumstances.

If you ask, 'Is it not true that, although someone continues to disobey for some time, his repentance can be accepted in the end?' I reply, 'Such disobedience happens because a man is overcome by desire, and his repentance is not planned in advance nor his life accordingly. God would pardon him and by His grace forgive him, because He knows how essentially weak man is. But a person who plans to disobey God for as long as he likes and then repent in the end is merely trying to deceive Him who can never be deceived, by taking his pleasure in advance and promising to repent later on. He may not in fact fulfil that promise, since renouncing pleasures and joys and trying to repent, is especially difficult in old age when the body is weak. People frequently postpone repentance until death comes to them or some obstacle prevents them so that they leave the world without having repented. They are like debtors who could discharge a future obligation straight away but keep postponing it until the due date falls, by which time their money is all gone and so the debt remains unpaid. Thus the best thing for people is to absolve themselves during their life in the constant expectation of death, desisting from sin and preferring righteousness.'

If you insist, 'Why do we then find people committing abominations and breaking the bounds of what is forbidden, even though the extent of their life has been concealed from them, and they must expect death at any time?' we say in reply, 'It is entirely characteristic that they should behave like this, since their frivolous nature and the hardness of their hearts prevents them desisting from or renouncing evil; such behaviour is not a result of bad design. A physician may sometimes prescribe a medicine for the benefit of a patient, but if the patient disobeys the instruction and does not refrain from what he was asked to refrain from and so fails to benefit from the prescription, that is not the fault of the physician but of the disobedient patient. If people, in spite of expecting death at any time, do not desist from sin they will be even more likely – given the certainty of long life – to commit the most terrible abominations. Thus, to expect death at any time is better than being certain of life over a long period. Besides, the expectation of death – although some people ignore it and gain no benefit – is wholesome for others who desist from disobedience, embrace good works and give their wealth and their valued possessions in charity to the poor and needy. It would not be just to deprive those who accept the blessing of this condition, because others waste their chances of benefiting from it.'

Telling the truth and lying
Consider the characteristics of propositions: truth is mixed with falsehood. If all statements were true, all people would be prophets and if all statements were lies, then they would be useless, superfluous and meaningless. As it is, they are sometimes truthful so that people may benefit from trustworthy advice or guard against mishaps, and frequently they are untruthful so that people do not rely on them completely.

Provision for human needs
Think of all the resources that can be found in the world suited to human use: earth for building, iron for industry, wood for ships, stones for grinding, copper for pots, silver for currency, jewels as assets, grain for nourishment, fruits for desserts, meat for food, fowls for delicacies, medicines for cures, beasts for carrying heavy loads, firewood for fuel, ashes for plaster, droppings for fertilizer, and the many more similarly useful materials one could list. Just think:

if a man entered a house to find there cupboards
filled with all human necessities and everything in
the house prepared for some purpose known to
human beings, would he imagine that all this had
happened haphazardly without deliberate arrangement?
How, then, can anyone put forward such an
argument about this world and all its provisions?

Provision requiring labour

Reflect on the Divine design evident in the way
these resources are provided for human needs.
Grain was created for people's food but they were
charged with grinding, kneading and baking it.
Cotton and camel wool were created for their
clothing but they were charged with carding,
spinning and weaving it. Trees were created to
produce fruits for them but they were charged with
planting, watering and looking after them. Herbs
and minerals were created for their medicine but
they were charged with picking, mixing and
processing them. There are many other examples.

See how human beings were spared the original
creation of things which were not within their
capabilities but were left the necessity of working on
them because that was in their best interests; if they
were spared the need to do any work, the whole
earth would be unable to tolerate the degree of
human insolence and arrogance which would lead

them to do things ruinous to themselves. If human
beings were given enough of everything they need,
they would find no joy or pleasure in living. Do you
not see that, if human beings were to arrive as
guests and be given all the food and service they
needed, they would grow weary of idleness and their
own souls would contend with them to find an
occupation? How much worse it would be if they
were given enough of everything throughout their
whole lives? The right way to arrange for all these
resources to be available for human beings, is to
make them work for them so that idleness does not
make people arrogant and proud; work prevents
them attempting to obtain what is impossible and, in
any case, unprofitable.

In his aphorisms, Ardashir said that bread and water
are the staff of human life. What he said is correct,
but reflect on the proportion evident in these two
essentials: man's need for water is greater than his
need for bread; he can bear hunger more than thirst;
the amount of water he needs is greater than the
amount of bread. He needs water to drink, to wash,
clean clothes and utensils, to water animals and
plants. Therefore, water is made freely available so
that people are spared the burden of seeking and
paying for it, whereas bread is available in limited
quantities and cannot be obtained except by skilled
work, intended to prevent people from indulging in

the wantonness and folly brought on by idleness.

Do you not understand why children are entrusted to a teacher when they are young, with immature minds, and educated so as to keep them from foolish frivolities which may bring them and their families great harm? This is human nature: if people were left unoccupied, they would surpass mere folly and wantonness and indulge in actions that would damage both themselves and their relatives. You can see, for example, how people behave who have grown up in affluence and luxury.

If people were not afflicted with physical suffering, would they desist from depravity? Would they humble themselves before God and show kindness to other people? Do you not observe that when afflicted with pain people become submissive and humble, earnestly seeking health and well-being from God and extending their hands in charity? If people did not feel pain when beaten, how would those in authority be able to punish debauchery and humble evildoers? How would children learn the various subjects and crafts? How would slaves be forced to submit to their masters and obey them? Is this not sufficient reproach for those who, like the Manichaeans, resentful of pain and suffering, deny God and divine order?

The necessity of male and female

If animals were born all male or all female, would not that mean the end of procreation of all animal species? Why should some newborn creatures be male and some female if not to ensure the continuity of reproduction? If you saw a picture of a man on a wall and someone came and said to you that this picture appeared by itself, nobody made it, would you not dismiss him scornfully? How can anyone rule out chance as the cause of a picture, which is like a shadow, without ruling it out as the cause of a real human being – a living, rational creature?

The limits of growth

Why do the bodies of animals, which are always feeding, not continue to grow for ever, but stop at an optimum limit, if not by Divine arrangement? Wise design determines that each species of animal should be of a certain size and not grow or shrink haphazardly; rather they grow until they reach their predetermined limit and then stop, although they continue to feed. If they were to go on growing they would be far too bulky and there would be no difference in, or limit to, their sizes. Human bodies, for instance, would be too large to walk or move and too cumbersome to exercise delicate crafts. Furthermore it would be difficult to arrange suitable clothing, bedding and shrouds. All this is prevented by making them stop growing when they reach their proper size.

Why individuals are not created alike

Why are individual human beings unlike one
another, when birds, beasts and other creatures are
much the same? You may observe a herd of gazelle
or a flock of sand-grouse and find them so similar
that you cannot distinguish one from the other.
Human beings, however, seem so different in their
shape and appearance that hardly any two are the
same in any one particular. The reason is that men
need to recognise each other by their features and
clothing, because of their interactions. No such
interaction takes place between animals; therefore,
they need not recognise one another as individuals
by their outward appearance. Do you not see that
birds and beasts are not harmed in any way by
looking alike? The situation is different with human
beings – twins are sometimes so similar that they
cause people difficulty in dealing with them: the
property of one may be given to the other, or one may
be punished for the misdeeds of the other. This even
happens sometimes to people with similar names, let
alone similar appearances. Who, other than Him
whose wisdom encompasses everything, could have
attended to such details, which scarcely enter our
minds, and made arrangements accordingly?

Beards for men, smooth faces for women

When man and woman reach physical maturity they
both have pubic hair. Why then does a beard appear

on a man's face and not a woman's, if not by that
divine arrangement, which disposes that a man
should guard and watch over a woman and that a
woman should be his wife to whom he is attracted
for intercourse? A man was given a beard because
of its dignified, awe-inspiring, and imposing
appearance, while a woman was not given one, so
that her face retains its freshness and beauty, a
great inducement to caressing and mating. Is it not
clear that creation displays perfect proportion,
giving and withholding according to what is good
and has purpose.

SIX

Philosophical Arguments

Philosophers have stated that Nature does nothing without purpose and does not fail to perfect each thing according to its kind. Experience testifies to this. But who has given Nature this wisdom and the ability to stop at the proper limit, neither exceeding nor falling short of it – something which rational minds cannot do, even after long experience? If you concede that Nature has the wisdom and power to do such things you have admitted what you used to deny, because this is the characteristic of the Creator; if you deny that Nature has wisdom and power then the plain truth will shine out clearly, declaring that these acts are done by the great wise Creator.

Abnormalities, not an argument against design

Some ancients have denied that there is deliberation and design in things, claiming that it was all accident and chance. Among them Diagoras and Epicurus, and some naturalists. Their arguments include natural occurrences such as a human being born misshapen, with one short hand, lacking one hand or with an extra finger. They claimed, 'This is proof that man did not come about by deliberation and design, but by accident and chance.' Aristotle and other philosophers have replied that a thing which happens by accident and chance is something that occurs once only, a certain accident that diverts Nature from its normal course, rather than something that runs according to the normal, continuous pattern in Nature. We find all species of animals following one pattern – a human child is born with two hands, two feet, five fingers and so on, like the vast majority of people. It is some ailment in the womb or in the tissues from which the foetus is composed that causes someone to be born different from this pattern, just as an imperfection in the wood or in a tool prevents the craftsman from making something correctly, as he intends. For the same reason, something similar to this may well happen in the offspring of animals where the young, most of which emerge healthy and sound, is born defective or with an extra limb or deformed. In the same way a defect can happen in manufacturing but we do not deduce from this that all artefacts are produced by accident or poor craftsmanship; individual defects in Nature do not lead us to the conclusion that all natural things happen by accident and chance. Thus the claim, founded on individual cases, that things happen by accident is incorrect and betrays ignorance.

Nor is suffering in the world

If you object, 'Why should such cases occur?' we reply that things are not determined by Nature so that the only explanation is, contrary to the claims of some people, that they are permitted deliberately by the design of the Creator. He made Nature run its normal course in most cases, deviating sometimes, however, because of certain accidents; this fact implies that Nature is commissioned and designed, needing the will and power of the Creator to reach its purpose and achieve its work. Some people have used occasional natural events, such as plague and mildew, hailstones and locusts, as pretexts to deny the Creator and intention. We reply, 'If the Creator does not control Nature, why do we not have even worse events, such as the sky falling to the ground, the earth sinking, the sun not rising at all, the springs and rivers running dry so that there is no water, the air becoming stale so that things ferment and rot, the oceans flowing over the land and submerging it? Why do even those things they cite, like plagues and locusts, not go on continuously, sweeping across the whole world instead of happening only occasionally and for a limited period?' Do you not see that the world is protected and preserved from great calamities which would bring the world to an end. At the same time, a few minor calamities happen to discipline men and put them on the right course; the calamity departs when they have all but despaired. Thus the coming of the calamity teaches them a lesson and its departure is a sign of the mercy of God.

Those who deny God may, like the Manichaeans, resent the adversities and calamities which afflict

people. Both argue that if the universe had a
merciful, clement Creator, these loathsome things
should not happen. However, such people are of the
opinion that human life in this world should be free
from all grief and distress. Had that been so, people
would be led to an arrogance and profligacy that
would not be healthy for their religion or their world.
Witness the many rulers who live in luxury and
ordinary people who live in affluence and security.
They strut about, some of them forgetting that they
are human beings subjected to a Master, or that
harm may touch them or adversity may afflict them.
They forget that they should show mercy to the
weak, help the poor, have pity on the afflicted and
show kindness to those in distress; but once they
feel the pain of affliction they learn their lesson and
begin to understand much they had not realised
before, and begin to do many of their duties. Those
who object to painful experiences are like children
who complain about bitter medicine, resent being
deprived of harmful food and hate discipline and
work. They love to be left to play and be idle and to
be allowed all sorts of food and drinks. They do not
know that idleness leads to bad education, conduct
and habits, and that harmful food leads to illness
and pain. They do not know that there is good in
discipline, and benefit in bitter medicine even if
they dislike them. If they argue, 'Why were human
beings not made infallible so that they would not

need to be jolted with such terrible events?' We say
that they could not then be praised for good deeds
nor deserve rewards. If they retort, 'What does it
matter if they are not praised or rewarded, so long as
they obtain the maximum pleasure and comfort?' We
say, 'Tell a person of sound body and mind to sit
there in comfort, provided with everything he needs,
without effort or merit and see if he will accept.' No,
you would find him more pleased and joyful with the
little he achieves by his own effort and activity than
with abundance that comes to him undeservedly.
Such is the bliss in the Hereafter. It comes to those
who have worked for it and deserved it. The bliss is
doubled in this way: great reward has been stored up
for them for the effort they make in this world, and
so ways are provided for them to gain this reward by
working. For such people, the pleasure and joy of
their reward will be complete.

If they argue, 'Do we not find that some people are
pleased with what they gain, even though they do
not deserve it? How can you deny that there will be
those who are happy to receive the bliss of the
Hereafter in the same way?' Our reply is this: 'If you
open this door to people they would indulge in
extreme wildness and savagery, doing indecent and
forbidden things. Who would refrain from any
indecency or make any effort to do any good if they
were certain of receiving bliss in the Hereafter? And

116

who would feel safe in person, family or wealth, if people felt secure from accountability and punishment? The harm caused by entering through that door would afflict people in this world, even before they go to the Hereafter. Moreover, it would be a complete denial of both justice and wisdom if both good and wicked people were all treated the same in this world and the Hereafter. It would be a cause for complaint that things were badly and improperly planned.'

Our opponents may find a way out. They cling to the following: calamities happen to people, good and wicked alike, or to the good while the wicked escape. They say, 'How can the plan of a wise Being allow this? What is the explanation?' We reply that, even though calamities happen to good and wicked indiscriminately, God Almighty has made them salutary for both: these calamities remind the good of God's blessing in their earlier days, and this leads them to thank Him and endure patiently; they restrain the wicked from persisting in sin and indecency. To be saved from such calamities is salutary for both: the righteous find joy in resuming their good lives; the wicked realise God's mercy and lenience with them, in keeping them safe undeservedly, and this induces them to show clemency and forgive those who have done them wrong.

You press further, 'Leave aside the misfortunes that happen to people, what do you have to say about the calamities that destroy the body altogether, like fire, flood or being engulfed by an earthquake? What is your explanation?' We say, 'God also makes these salutary for both the good and the wicked: the righteous have the consolation of leaving this world, its obligations and troubles; the wicked have some of their sins rectified and are prevented from further sins.'

In short, the Creator disposes all things in a good and beneficial way, just as a subtle craftsman will employ a tree uprooted by the wind or a broken palm for all sorts of purposes. The wise Disposer employs in a truly beneficial way all the calamities and misfortunes which afflict human beings. If you say, 'Why should such things happen to people at all?' we reply, 'To stop them relying on the continuance of that security which encourages the wicked to trust in sinful things and slackens the efforts of the righteous to do good.' These two attitudes predominate among people living in comfort and ease, and disastrous events make them humble and rouse them to do what is right. If they are free from such calamities they persist in their wickedness and sin, just as they did at the dawn of time until it became necessary to exterminate them with the Flood and purge the earth of their presence.

Nor are death and extinction, or natural disasters, or injustice

Unbelievers also resent any suggestion of planning in death and extinction. They take the view that people should live in this world eternally free from troubles. We should perhaps follow this view to its logical conclusion and see where it leads. Imagine: if all people who came into this world were to remain there with none of them dying, would not the world become too small for them? There would not be sufficient houses, fields and jobs for them all. And if they did not die gradually, would not fierce competition over those things lead to wars and bloodshed? And what would life be like for them if they were to be born but not die? In addition to this, greed, covetousness and cruelty would dominate because, if people were sure that they would not die, nobody would be content with anything gained nor would they find pleasure in giving to others or receiving from them. Furthermore, they would get bored with life and everything in it, just as someone who lives to a great age wishes for death and to be released from this world.

If it were argued that they should be spared misfortune and suffering so that they do not wish to die, we have already described the arrogance and cruelty this would lead to, a state of affairs good neither for their religion nor their world. If it were

argued further that they should not be able to
procreate so that houses and jobs would not be too
scarce, we would answer that, if God brought into
this world only one generation which did not
procreate then this would deprive most people of
being born and enjoying the blessings of God and
the gifts He gives them in this world and the next. If
they then say that He could create in that single
generation as many as He could create to the end of
the world, we return to the scarcity of buildings and
jobs. Besides, people unable to procreate would not
enjoy relationships by blood and marriage nor get
necessary assistance from them, nor enjoy bringing
up children and being pleased with them. This
proves that whatever our imagination may be able to
grasp beyond the existing plan of the Creator is
badly wrong, both in conception and formulation.

Someone might object to the idea of Divine planning
on another ground, namely: 'How can there be
planning, when we see both mighty and weak in this
world, the strong oppressing others and causing
resentment, while the weak are oppressed and suffer
in poor conditions? We find the righteous poor and
afflicted and the wicked healthy and affluent, and
people indulging in improper and unlawful
behaviour without being swiftly punished. If there
were design in this world one would expect that the
righteous would thrive and the wicked be deprived;

the strong would be prevented from oppressing the weak and those who behave despicably would be punished sooner.' In answer to this we say, 'If this were the case there would be no place for the trials of life by which people can distinguish themselves, nor would they make the effort to do good and righteous deeds, seeking and trusting in God's promised reward. They would sink to the status of beasts, ruled by the stick and the carrot alternately, to make them behave. Nobody would act in the certain expectation of eventual reward or punishment: they would lose their human status and assume the lower one of animals, aware only of what they can see and acting only on the spur of the moment. In addition, the righteous would do good only for the sake of an affluent livelihood in this world and refrain from injustice and impropriety only because they expect immediate punishment. Thus people's actions would only be for the present, without that trust in the rewards of God which deserves the recompense of eternal joy in the Hereafter.

Besides riches and poverty, health and illness do not always occur according to expectation, sometimes they do and we find righteous people given abundant wealth by Divine plan. In any case, people do not believe that only the wicked thrive and the righteous go without, and so prefer wickedness to righteousness. Moreover we often find that the wicked are quickly punished when they have exceeded all limits and have become very dangerous to themselves and others. Witness the drowning of Pharaoh, the Israelites getting lost in the wilderness and the killing of Belshezzar. That some wicked people do not receive their punishment in this world, and some good ones have their rewards delayed until the Hereafter for reasons that are hidden from human beings, does not disprove the existence of planning. That earthly kings act in a somewhat similar fashion does not disprove that they make plans; their postponement of certain things and advancement of others is rather a part of correct and proper planning.'

We ask further, 'If comparison suggests and evidence proves that everything has a wise and powerful Creator, what could prevent Him from planning His creation?' To give a comparison, it is wrong to assert that a craftsman could neglect his craft, except for one of these three reasons: inability, ignorance or wickedness. All of these are impossible for the Eternal Creator (Glory be to Him!), for an incompetent person could not create such great and wonderful things, an ignorant person could not conceive the wise perfection of them and a wicked person would not take the trouble to create them. This being so it follows inevitably that the Creator of all we see plans it, even if we do not grasp the exact nature of such planning and how it proceeds. Much of what kings plan is not understood by commoners, nor do they know why it is so, because they do not know the minds and secrets of kings. If they were told why, they would pronounce it justified and in accordance with their expectations and experience.

All things indicate the wisdom of the Creator

If you doubted the strength of some medicine or food and it subsequently became clear to you (on two or three counts) that it was strong or weak, would you not accept the evidence and banish doubt from your mind? Why can you not accept that the world is created and planned, with all these many proofs and innumerable others? If half the things in the world made us uncertain as to its perfection, it would be neither judicious nor proper to assume that the whole world was a matter of chance because the appropriateness and perfection of the other half would prevent a hasty conclusion in this matter. How much more so then, when everything in the world if examined closely, is found to be so completely perfect that not a single thing that we can imagine can be as ideal and perfect as what has actually been created?

Do you know the name of the universe in Greek? It is *kosmos*, which means 'ornament'; and it is claimed that Pythagoras gave it that name, which was subsequently used by other philosophers and ordinary people. Would a wise philosopher give it such a name if it were not for its order and proportion. They were not content to call it 'order and proportion' but used 'ornament' to indicate that, in addition to its complete perfection, it is extremely beautiful and splendid. It is amazing that some people, who refuse to believe that a medication could be wrong even though they see the doctors regularly making mistakes, believe that the world came into being by chance when they can see nothing accidental about it! Do not be surprised by the boorish and uncouth Dosi[?], who was ignorant of the part played by Wisdom in Creation and lashed it with abuse. However, you should be surprised by the abandoned Mani who claimed that he had been given knowledge of the occult, yet was blind to the indications of Wisdom in Creation, who attributed it to bungling and branded its Creator with ignorance. Exalted is the Wise and Generous Lord, high above their assertions!

The extent of human knowledge of God; hidden in essence, obvious in Creation

Even more surprising are those who deny God because they expect to perceive with their senses something which cannot be perceived by the mind. When they cannot do this, they resort to rejection and denial, saying, 'Why should the mind not apprehend Him?' We say, 'He is beyond the capacity of the mind. Sight cannot perceive what is beyond its scope. If you see a stone rising in air you know that someone has thrown it. Sight can only see the stone rising, and the fact that someone threw it is not a visual but a mental inference because the mind correctly judges that the stone could not rise in the air by itself. Do you not see how the sight does not exceed its competence? The mind, likewise, is incapable of going beyond its own level of knowledge of the Creator.' They then argue, 'So we do not comprehend Him?' We say, 'Yes, you do: our level of understanding is one of affirmation only and not of full comprehension, even as a person knows that he has a soul, without seeing it or perceiving it by any of the senses.'

Another example is to be found in the indivisibility of a point. The mind inevitably asserts its existence in that a line must begin from a point, yet it cannot be perceived by the senses because a point observed by sense is inevitably divisible. Scholars of geometry teach that a perfect triangle is a mental abstraction. A drawn triangle, however, with lines that can be perceived by the senses cannot be free from imperfection however meticulous our attempt to draw it. Accordingly, we say that the mind knows the Creator from deductions and proofs but not from sense and comprehension. In short, the mind knows Him through the need to affirm Him, but not through the need to comprehend His attributes. Unbelievers go on, 'How is it that a feeble servant is required to know Him when a subtle mind cannot comprehend Him?' We reply, 'Servants are charged only with that which is within their capacity, that is, to believe in Him and act according to His orders; they are not required to comprehend Him and His attributes. In the same way, a king does not command his subjects to know whether he is tall or short or fair or dark, but only to submit to his authority and not exceed the limits he sets.' If a man came before the portal of a king and demanded, 'Present yourself to me, so that I can know you more deeply, otherwise I will not listen to what you say,' would you not admit that he deserved punishment? In the same way, the person who will not believe in the Creator until he comprehends His very nature is also subject to His wrath.

They continue, 'Is it not the case that we describe Him when we say, "He is the Mighty, the Wise, the Generous?" ' We say, 'These are all adjectives of affirmation, acknowledgement and consent, but not adjectives of comprehension. We know He is wise, but we do not comprehend the essence of His wisdom. Neither do we comprehend the meaning of "powerful" and "generous" and other such adjectives. We see the sky but do not know its essence, and we see the ocean but do not know where it ends, but He is infinitely above all comparisons. All analogies, even though they may lead the mind towards knowing Him, ultimately fall short.'

Then they ask, 'Why do we hold such different opinions about Him then?' We reply, 'Because our conjectures fall short of appreciating the extent of His greatness, and exceed mere affirmation in seeking to know Him; we try to comprehend Him, though we are unable to comprehend even lesser realities. Why, for instance, have there been so many opinions concerning the sun, which we see shining on the world every day without knowing its nature? Philosophers have disagreed in describing it. Anaximenes said it was a hollow celestial sphere, full of fire, with a mouth that gushes out heat and radiance; Xenophanes said it was a mixture of fiery elements agitated by moist vapour, whereas Anaximenes said it was a flaming cloud. Philolaus the Pythagorean, on the other hand, said it was a glass body which absorbs the fiery nature of the universe and sends its rays to the earth. The Stoics said it was a gentle essence which rises from the sea; Plato said it was numerous pieces of fire assembled together, whereas Aristotle said it was a fifth element in addition to the four we know. They also disagreed about its shape. Anaximenes said it was like a broad sheet, the Stoics said it was like a rolling ball, and Aristotle said something similar. They disagreed, moreover, about its size. Anaximandros said it was as large as the Earth, Anaximenes said it was smaller, whereas Anaxagoras stated it was bigger than a large island; Proclus said it was as large as a man's foot, while scholars of geometry said it was 170 times larger than the earth. The disagreement in their views about the sun, which can be seen by the eye and perceived by the senses, is proof that they did not know its real nature. Thus, if the sun, which is seen by the eye and perceived by the senses, has baffled minds and rendered them unable to realise its nature, how much more would be the case with that which cannot be perceived by the senses and is hidden from conjecture?'

They press further, 'Why did He conceal Himself?' We respond, 'He did not conceal Himself by a device which He contrived, as someone conceals himself from people with doors and curtains. What we mean by saying he is "hidden" is that he is too subtle for our capability of conjecture, even as the soul is too subtle to be perceived by sight.' To ask, 'Why is He too subtle and too exalted?' would be a meaningless question because it is only fitting that the Cause of everything should surpass and be

above everything. There are only four ways in which
we can seek to know anything: the first is to ponder,
'Does it exist or not?' The second is to know its
essence; the third is to know its structure and
characteristics; and the fourth is to know its cause.
A creature cannot really know the Creator in any of
these ways, apart from knowing that He exists. Full
knowledge of the nature of God – what He is and
how He is – cannot be given to a creature. The
cause of His existence does not apply to the Creator
because He is the Cause of everything, and is not
caused by anything. For human beings to know that
God exists does not require that they know what He
is and how He is. In the same way, their knowledge
that the soul exists does not require that they know
what and how it is. The same applies to other
spiritual and immaterial things.

They complain, 'You have been so extravagant in
describing how knowledge falls short of Him, that it
is as if He were not known at all.' We say, 'That is
true, if you mean that the mind desires to know His
nature and to comprehend Him. In another respect,
when you seek knowledge of Him by sufficient
proofs or indications, He is nearer than everything
near to you.' Aristotle gives a similar solution in
his book called *Metaphysics*; he describes Him by
saying 'He is near-far.' On the one hand, He is not
hidden from anyone; on the other He is like a

mystery which no one can comprehend. The mind is like this. It is obvious in its operations, yet hidden in its essence. When such statements are made about the mind, no one should refuse to make similar statements about the mind's Creator and Maker.

This brings us to the end of the evidence of Creation and design we have included in this book. It is a little out of a great amount, a small part of a mighty whole. Full knowledge is with the Wise, All-Knowing Creator. Many devout and abiding thanks are due to Him.